THE
MEMORIES

THE MEMORIES
1961–JFK–1963

of CECIL STOUGHTON, the President's photographer
and Major General CHESTER V. CLIFTON, the President's military aide,
narrated by HUGH SIDEY

W · W · NORTON & COMPANY
New York · London

DEDICATIONS

The 1,065 days of the presidency of John Fitzgerald Kennedy were my golden days, filled with the special joy of living and working with young and vital people who had found a cause beyond themselves.

Those days were not without personal sacrifice. Prolonged periods of absence from my family were necessary. My wife, Faith, and children, Bill, Jamie, and Sharon carried on cheerfully and gracefully even though they could not share in my special experience. It is for them that I do this book, to show my profound affection and let them in this way share those days. Without their love, faith, and a belief in what I was doing, the separation would have been difficult. This, then, is my legacy to them.

Cecil Stoughton

My minor contribution is dedicated to my wife, Anne, for whose love and support I am forever grateful.

Ted Clifton

Cecil Stoughton, Ted Clifton, and the narrator especially dedicate these pictures and words to the Kennedy family, hoping that they will be a tribute to John F. Kennedy's memory, and a source of pleasure for Jacqueline, Caroline, and John, Jr.

Hugh Sidey

First published as a Norton paperback 1980.

Library of Congress Cataloging in Publication Data

Stoughton, Cecil.
   The memories of Cecil Stoughton, the President's photographer, and Major General Chester V. Clifton, the President's military aide.

   Cover title: The memories: JFK, 1961–1963.
   1. Kennedy, John Fitzgerald, Pres. U.S., 1917–1963—Portraits, caricatures, etc.   2. Kennedy family—Portraits, caricatures, etc.   I. Clifton, Chester V.
II. Sidey, Hugh.   III. Title.   IV. Title: The memories: JFK, 1961–1963.
E842.5.S86   973.922′092′4 [B]   73–12021

ISBN 0-393-00985-8

Photographs Copyright © 1961, 1962, 1963, by Cecil Stoughton

Text and captions Copyright © 1973, by Hugh Sidey, Chester V. Clifton, Cecil Stoughton

Published simultaneously in Canada by
Penguin Books Canada Ltd,
2801 John Street, Markham, Ontario L3R 1B4.

Printed in the United States of America

5 6 7 8 9 0

DESIGNED BY EMMA LANDAU

OVERLEAF:
12:51 P.M., January 20, 1961. John F. Kennedy became the thirty-fourth President of the United States. In 15 degree weather, Chief Justice Earl Warren administered the Oath of Office.

INTRODUCTION

By HUGH SIDEY

How easily the memories march out even after ten years. The least signal and there we are again reliving the days of John F. Kennedy. Like old soldiers we gather and tell the stories over. Do you remember Inaugural Night and his tour of the festivities through the banks of snow? And finally how he stood on the White House steps alone in the cold. He turned and gave a few of us a good night then stepped through the door with his hands in his pockets to start his special adventure.

There was the evening after the Soviet Union had put a man in space that Kennedy pushed back his chair from the Cabinet table and ran his fingers through his hair, despairing that the United States could ever catch up. But then there was the day almost three years later when he stood at Cape Canaveral beside Dr. Werner von Braun. He rocked on the balls of his feet looking at the towering first stage of the Saturn Rocket that would put Americans on the moon, far ahead of the Russians in the space race. That moment, hands still in his pockets, he glowed.

Do you remember when Kennedy journeyed overseas for the first time, stopping in Paris on the way to Vienna? There was a special pride in the First Couple. They exuded enthusiasm. They always said the right thing. There was the sense of adventure. Then came the sweet and sour hours of the Vienna summit with Nikita Khrushchev. Jackie listened to the soaring voices of the Vienna Boys Choir in morning mass. John Kennedy came out of his last meeting with the Soviet leader glum and downcast. He had heard his adversary bang the table and roar that Berlin was like a bone in his throat.

Later that year there was the time of the Berlin Wall and the chilling confrontation. And then there was the Nuclear Test-Ban Treaty and his extra dimension of pride in that achievement.

The days of the Cuban Missile Crisis form a special interlude when his inner circle devised one of the most sensible power maneuvers in the postwar period and executed it with skill. A deeper, more thoughtful President lifted off the White House grounds in a helicopter the morning when the Soviet ships turned back and Khrushchev agreed to our demands. He rested in Virginia profoundly satisfied for perhaps the first time in his Presidency.

And remember Kennedy's tour of Berlin in 1963 when millions turned out to roar their affection and listen to him praise their courage in living in the shadow of the wall. And don't forget the day in Ireland at Wexford when the crowd began to sing "The Soldiers' Song." The tenor voices lifted in the gathering darkness and a few of us up close thought we saw Kennedy's eyes fill with moisture. But his voice was firm and his humor was intact. He introduced all his staff members as true Irishmen, no matter what their legitimate heritage. At that hour, at that place everyone was truly an Irishman.

Almost every moment of those 1,065 days is grasped by someone and stored away carefully to be savored when the news grows bad and concern rises. We remember so clearly the bursts of laughter, the irreverence, the muttered cuss words, the inevitable dignity and politeness, the love of language and new thoughts, the concern about showing courage, the pervasive idea that mankind's calling was the pursuit of excellence. No one moment by itself means that much, perhaps, but when put together in our minds by some natural process which we don't fully understand, they form a mosaic of profound human appeal.

What did John Kennedy's Presidency really mean? I couldn't tell you now. And I'm deeply suspicious of those who have figured it out so tidily already. I am particularly intrigued by those who are mustering their credentials and with long faces have begun to dismantle the legend. What legend? Well, of course, they say—Camelot. But who raises that image really but the people beyond the fringe who never saw much from inside? There were the times of glitter and special glamour. But for every hour of that, there were many more of tedious, grueling, and agonizing work that nobody ever heard of or cared about. So, I say, let the revisionists march up and down their hills. They can study their boxscores of bills passed and not passed, treaties signed and dollars appropriated, and their criticisms of programs initiated. That is a favorite and easy journalistic measure of presidential progress. But it happens to be somewhat out of date. Forty years ago, in the New Deal, when the needs of the nation could be measured quantitatively in terms of houses, meals, clothes, there was something to this device. But the spiritual needs of today can't be assayed in metric tons or with price tags or by units. The special quality of John Kennedy that still defies those who would diminish him is that he touched something in the American spirit and it lives on in memory.

This is no proposal that we hail Kennedy as the greatest President of the century. This is a memory in pictures and in modest rations of prose. It is an effort to capture those interludes of pleasure and pain which we endured with Kennedy and which marked us all.

I run into the kids in college today who were in grade school back on the day Kennedy was shot. They watched in uncomprehending fascination as the drama unfolded on their television screens. It seared them. Perhaps they were not uncomprehending at all. Maybe in a very basic way they know more than we did. Whatever, they now raise John Kennedy into their special pantheon. And those of us who were old enough to know him and those even older who could doubt him—well, again, the old joys, the old fascinations, swirl up when we see those familiar pictures, when we happen to hear the voice.

If the pleasure of his company—as his friend Paul (Red) Fay put it so beautifully—could be analyzed I suspect what we might find, through another of those strange human processes, is that we discovered a little more pleasure in ourselves. Courage became a bit more fashionable. We discovered new recesses of chivalry. We got the idea that adventure was not dead. Kennedy urged the space missions and in doing so recalled Frank O'Connor, an Irish writer who talked of his own boyhood, how he and his friends would roam the countryside and, coming to a high wall, would throw their hats over the wall so they then would have to climb it and drop into the unknown on the other side. The critics would say, of course, it was exactly this sort of romance that led us astray. We went to the moon and spent $25 billion, while our country rotted in Watts and Hough and Harlem. There is something to that argument—but not much. There is nothing in human experience to assure that resources not expended on space would have found their way into human concerns. Indeed, there is more evidence to suggest quite the opposite—that bright moments of adventure, of achievement, open minds and hearts far more than the dismal seasons of stagnation. What if in these last years of national anguish we had not had the moon spectaculars? What if we had stood rooted in our ruins and been forced to watch the Soviet Union lead us into the solar system?

John Kennedy in his brief stewardship caught some buried resonance of the American spirit. He had enough of the old buccaneer in him to be suspicious of do-gooders and fond of professional "pols" with all of their visible flaws. He was reverent about the fundamentals of the nation and in awe of the giants who had walked the White House corridors before him. Yet there always was the understanding of how limited we were, how ridiculous our efforts must seem to the presiding force, whoever or whatever it might be. There was in Kennedy the notion that our time was fleeting and the only thing that would eventually be measured was whether each man did his best with his natural endowments. Thus, steeped in the history which he loved and read, Kennedy sought new challenge and adventure over almost every wall he encountered in his brief wanderings as President.

That, I guess, is why we take this trouble to remember him after ten years. This book will not even touch all the issues or the incidents of his years. It is, basically, a collection of silver nitrate vignettes, those fragments snipped off during his days and nights in the White House. Along with them are brief prose pictures designed more to enhance the mood of the pictures than to give any final definition of Kennedy's Presidency.

Yet, this compendium of Kennedy-the-man is surely the best glimpse of his special grace as yet published. Much in these pages will be familiar. A lot is new. Kennedy was the first television President. He invaded the living rooms of America with no hesitation. He showed himself and his family off when it was both necessary and natural. And so, in a way, we all claimed him. The magic comes back now through the camera of Cecil Stoughton and the eyes of Chester V. (Ted) Clifton. They were rather an unlikely pair. Clifton was an Army General who became Kennedy's Military Aide. He brought Stoughton, then an Army Lieutenant, to the White House to provide a visual record. Neither man was just sure on that cold Inaugural Day what lay ahead of him. But it did not take many days for them to discover the great fascination of residing near the center of power, the further enchantment of seeing a young, fresh figure grapple with the immense problems brought to him. Finally, there was the lasting affection which they both developed for the man and his wife. They were there when the State Dining Room was filled with its most important guests and there was wit and eloquence. They were there, too, when the others had gone and only a husband and wife and children were left, saying and doing and feeling like so many others in America.

And they were both in the motorcade that fateful day in Dallas.

Listen, then, to the humor of understatement, to the dry chuckle, to the clap of the hands, the slightly off-key voice giving a tune for the kids' dance, those small moments which intruded into the presidential world, which stopped the great gears in their tracks. Maybe right there we come closest to the meaning of John Kennedy to this nation. Or maybe it comes later, toward the end, as the family sits in the back of the White House viewing the Black Watch, tiny arms circling their father's shoulders.

So often, so carelessly the essence of the Kennedy years used to be dismissed as "style." Kennedy was "stylish" to use the term of political scientist James David Barber. He did look and act well. But he also had "style," which Barber defined as something which stems from the character of a man. It is what he knows and what he feels, it is how experience has formed and tempered him. It is, in the end, how he deals with his fellow man. And that, too, is what this book is all about.

THE CHIEF EXECUTIVE,
THE COMMANDER IN CHIEF,
THE POLITICIAN

"The pay is pretty good and you can walk home to lunch."

... JFK

"When you are around here you have to eat fast, read fast, think fast, and sleep fast or else you won't get anything done." Ted Clifton remembers John Kennedy's wry observation of the presidential pace. The world flowed through the Oval Office every twenty-four hours and it didn't really wait for anyone, not even the President. He climbed on that surging current of human affairs and went with it, managing it as best he could, but never yielding or it would have swept over him. I asked him once if he had trouble sleeping in that swift world knowing that each morning was apt to bring a new crisis. Kennedy said he had worried at first, but soon saw the folly in this. He couldn't control the world. He did his best to set things straight during the day, then left it to others during the night. He greeted each dawn with a sense of adventure—and a renewed charge of energy.

The Kennedy day began with the newspapers. Clifton often answered his summons about 8 A.M. and occasionally found him stretched out in bed, breakfast tray pushed aside, and the demolished pages of the morning papers strewn around him. He consumed five or six papers in his own special method of scanning, halting, exclaiming, studying. He tore out the stories that he wanted checked. He stored other fragments of fact in his head and he turned them into questions later in the day. He found in the papers almost as much of interest as he found in the intelligence reports brought in by Clifton. In the intelligence analyses there were often facts that didn't get into the papers. But in the papers there was drama and mood and some of the best opinion, which often the intelligence reports had none of. "Where did this come from," Kennedy would sometimes bark at Clifton, whose job at such moments was simply to know every answer to every question, which, of course was impossible—and Kennedy knew that too. "Listen to what Lippmann says," he would declare. Or he would wave one of the fragments of newsprint and order, "Get me more."

His restless eyes could devour twelve hundred words or more a minute. And he was an expert at reading between the lines. His background in journalism, his continuing fascination with editors and publications gave him a rare instinct with which he could spot special prejudices, unerringly identify the sources of certain stories. More often than not his morning reading was a good-humored interlude. He gathered up in his glances, if there was time, a mixture of the substantive issues, the human affairs, sports and gossip. Very little that was juicy escaped his eye. "What's wrong with *Life,*" he once asked when that magazine first began to feel the heat of television. "I don't believe the pictures of the girls are as good as they used to be," he said answering his own question.

Kennedy's penchant for reading the papers of course sent ripples throughout the Administration. In self-defense, not only his aides but his Cabinet officers and generals had to get into the newspaper act.

When Maxwell Taylor was appointed Special Military Assistant to the President he came along with Clifton and McGeorge Bundy one morning. As they strode through the White House corridors, Taylor asked Clifton what the President generally asked about. "He asks about what he reads," Clifton answered. "Put me on the newspaper summary list," said Taylor, assuming that the President must have somebody digest all that print for him and serve it up in tidy increments. "We don't have a summary," said Clifton casually. "We read newspapers like mad."

Aside from the sheer pleasure of savoring the world events as seen through the eyes of reporters, Kennedy had another reason for his search for facts. He knew that Presidents could easily isolate themselves. He had read about the problems other Presidents had had in getting the truth. He learned from the Bay of Pigs just how blinded a man can be surrounded by experts. Not only was the printed word a way to reach out beyond his doors, but it was a compendium of proper skepticism.

From bed and newspapers Kennedy moved to his office in the West Wing. It was in the Oval Office that the real work of the Presidency was shouldered. Here the meetings with the staff members were held. The Cabinet and National Security Council members assembled there in ad hoc committees to tackle crises or domestic programs and plans. He held meetings of the full Cabinet and the full National Security Council in the Cabinet Room, when tradition or crisis demanded it. But that was not the way Kennedy liked to work. He found often that the issues were so specialized that to assemble the entire Cabinet or NSC was a waste of a lot of manpower and time.

As Clifton remembers it, almost no one came away from a meeting with Kennedy without feeling that the visitor had found a special audience. Even the ceremonial visitors sometimes found themselves asked the most important questions. Clifton remembers with amusement the morning a Prime Minister from a small and remote African country paid an official visit. He settled beside the President for a few minutes of small talk which usually prefaced the more serious subjects on the agenda. Suddenly, Kennedy turned to him and asked, "What would you do about Berlin?" Stunned, the man hesitated. But detecting Kennedy's sincerity, he gave his opinion, the President nodding as he talked. Later, the visiting head of state left the White House buoyantly. "What would my opinion mean to him?" he asked. Then, not stopping for an answer, he said to Clifton, "That is the most flattering thing that has ever happened to me. And to think that I came here to talk about the economics of wildlife preservation in our African country."

Bookkeepers, administrative experts, and flow charts horrified Kennedy. He had a system of working, but it was his own, designed to fit the human dimensions which he proscribed. Long before, he had concluded that government was not necessarily a tidy or efficient operation. It was an operation of men, complete with all the frustrations that men can impose on one another. Sometimes he assigned two men to do a single job. Sometimes because he didn't remember that he had done it. But often, he had a purpose—to get two sets of conclusions about the same problem. He worked with the doors of his office open (that meant the back door was open too). This was another way in which he battled the institutional isolation of the Presidency. In particular, he wanted a steady flow of journalists whom he felt would bring in fresh views from outside and who would not be afraid to talk about them. Often Press Secretary Pierre Salinger would poke his head into the Oval Office and be startled to see a reporter talking with the President. Sometimes a Cabinet officer would be coming down the hall past the President's office and catch sight of one of his underlings with the President. At first it was rather unsettling to those confronted by these unexpected scenes. But quickly it became known that this was Kennedy's way.

Though Kennedy never made it a public issue, he was concerned about conserving his energy. Going too long without rest he felt affected one's temper and judgment. He was determined when he entered the White House to prevent fatigue when at all possible. He institutionalized an after-lunch nap.

On typical days there was provision for a swim in addition to rest. Sometimes he combined these indulgences with a bit of low-key work. More than one guest in his office was swept along with him into the heated swimming pool where they would paddle up and down discussing whatever business they had between them. Sometimes the discussions would go on in Kennedy's bedroom as hot packs were applied to his back and lunch was brought in on a tray. When lunch was over and the conversation had gone as far as the President wanted it to go, he would begin to settle himself in for a bit of sleep and the visitor would be bid good-by.

Humor was such an integral part of Kennedy that it became almost a part of the White House routine. There was hardly any time, no matter how serious the business, that he did not have a laugh or two lurking beneath the surface. He could gently jibe himself and his friends, and certainly his family.

Clifton was in a National Security Council meeting one day watching Bobby Kennedy fidget in impatience behind the President's chair. Though not an official member of the NSC, Bobby was a regular participant. From his spot along the wall Bobby kept handing notes to the President, who ignored them. The meeting went on without a look or a nod toward the Attorney General. Finally almost everybody else had been called on except Bobby. Then the President, with a dry chuckle, said, "I've asked almost everybody's opinion. I have the feeling that there is a very restless Attorney General. We will now entertain his comments."

After Bobby had been described in the press as "the second most powerful man in the nation," a visitor in Kennedy's office was startled when the President answered the phone, listened a minute, covered the speaker, said, "The second most powerful man in America is on the line." The President listened again, looked up laughing, and said, "He wants to know who is number one."

To survive the long hours of tedium that are necessarily a part of running a machine as big and cumbersome as the U.S. government, Kennedy had a number of rituals of relief with his staff. One that always brought a silent laugh to Clifton was the high sign delivered in the middle of a ponderous discussion. The Military Aide would hurry to the President's side and be handed a folded piece of paper. He would take it briskly, step back, open it, then take a minute to study the message. It often was blank. What that meant was that the President wanted a cigar. Clifton would go to the supply of cigars, slip one in an envelope or behind a book and deliver the goods with full military bearing.

Hardly a day was complete without a ceremony or two somewhere on the premises. Debate has raged in each of the modern Presidencies as to whether the President should be relieved of this kind of duty. But no President has yet felt he could abandon these chores, which range from listening to championship high school bands to accepting the traditional Thanksgiving turkey from the Turkey Growers of America. How many high school bands are there? Thousands. And how many parents of those kids are there? Millions. And what does that mean in political terms? Votes. The same progression can be applied to the Turkey Growers, the milk producers, and so on, hence any suggestion that the Rose Garden traditions be abandoned necessarily gets a hard eye in the Oval Office.

Kennedy had a horror of hats and would seldom put one on in public where he could be photographed. When the hat industry complained bitterly he conceded and began to carry a hat, but it rarely got on his head. He had an even greater horror of being forced to don the unorthodox headdresses of visiting delegations. One day, when preparing to meet a group of Indian chiefs in the Rose Garden, a worried Kennedy asked Clifton what was about to happen. "They're not going to give me a bunch of feathers to wear, are they?" Assured that they were not, the presidential sense of humor reasserted itself. "And General," he said, recalling former Army-Indian hostilities and the Cavalry uniforms of frontier days, "I've got a suggestion. Don't wear your blue uniform when we go out to meet those Indians."

If Indians gave the President pause, politics never did. Clifton expressed his concern one morning to Kennedy about the approaching retirement ceremony for Air Force General Emmett (Rosie) O'Donnell. Among the guests invited to the ceremony was Senator Barry Goldwater, shaping up as Kennedy's likely opponent in 1964. "What are we going to do," asked Clifton. "You've got a picture out there that every photographer has been waiting for—you and Senator Goldwater." Kennedy grinned. "Look, General," he said, "politics is my thing, not yours. Watch me." Kennedy strode into the sunlight, conducted the retirement ceremony with good humor. Meantime Goldwater feeling a little self-conscious himself hovered on the edge of the group. At the end, Kennedy called him. "Barry, come over here," The President grabbed the Senator's hand in a firm grip, took hold of his elbow with the other hand. The cameras clacked away. "Mr. President, turn me loose," Goldwater finally laughed.

In the Kennedy days the nuclear shadow still followed the Presidency. The Soviet Union was suspect. The possibility of nuclear war was still discussed in the Sunday supplements as something that man might be fool enough to unleash. From this nuclear consciousness came the stories of the "black bag" or the "football," the pouch containing the President's codes and instructions for launching missiles and bombers against an enemy in an emergency. Some stories were true, some not. There was in fact a warrant officer assigned to carry the codes. The man was required to be within one minute's distance of the President at all times. When the President traveled, the "bag man" could be spotted in the presidential party always trying desperately to blend into the background. Foreign newsmen and photographers were more fascinated with this scenario than Americans, and they inevitably picked out the bag man, reporting in detail his looks and his actions.

One overly enthusiastic writer concocted an account that the bag man sat outside the President's bedroom door every night, all night. A concerned Kennedy confronted Clifton with it. "Say," he asked, "is there really a guy outside my bedroom door all night long?" No, he was assured, the fellow resided in the basement of the White House. He could travel the distance to the President's side in the alloted time if necessary.

Keeping staff and Cabinet, generals and congressional leaders informed of his plans was a major part of Kennedy's work and he insisted that his staff members get together among themselves so that each knew what the other was doing. He urged his Cabinet officers to consult each other when they tackled problems which cut across traditional jurisdictional lines. Kennedy did not subscribe to the old Franklin Roosevelt theory that friction and competition between his men would improve performance. He was particularly careful not to offend his Vice-President. The President gave orders to Clifton to keep LBJ up to date on all White House events, to be certain that he was included in the meetings on subjects which would concern the Vice-President. It was not always the easiest thing to do, as Clifton found out. Johnson was accustomed to doing just what he wanted to do and when he wanted to do it (like flying off to his ranch in Texas when suddenly struck with the urge to look at his prize bulls or to walk along the hilltops at sunset). "LBJ used to raise hell when he wouldn't hear about important meetings," says Clifton. "But sometimes he wasn't in town." Despite the difficulties, the effort paid off; relations between Johnson and Kennedy were about as smooth as they could be between two such strong men. And JFK was appreciative of what Johnson did for him. "Lyndon is doing one hell of a job," he once mused to Clifton. "It is not my style, but he is doing it the way he knows best."

Kennedy's interest in military matters was of special gratification to Clifton and Stoughton. It is a curious turn of Kennedy's character that, as a man of peace who wanted nothing so much as to lead the United States into a time of tranquility, he was abnormally fascinated with the men and the machines of war. Kennedy was particularly intrigued with his own communications. In the early days of the nuclear age, he was obligated to consult with Great Britain and Canada before taking any nuclear action if time were available. Consequently, the White House Signal people from the Army were constantly working on communications with our allies. First there was a connection made to 10 Downing Street and it was tested time and again. One time, checking it himself to see if the military assurances of communications speed were accurate, he got the Prime Minister out of bed. When the "hot line" was put in to de Gaulle, he left it to his aides to do the testing. Having read in *Parade* magazine of a suggestion made that we have a "hot line" to Moscow, he directed that Clifton and

On the stump in 1962, Kennedy performs in his role as Democratic party leader.

the communicators work on it until it was finally established by teletype between the Pentagon Command Center and the Kremlin. The world-wide command communications system run by the Department of Defense is able to get all the senior commanders in the world on the line within two or three minutes, and Kennedy once startled his Air Force commander in Alaska by trying his hot line and explaining rather apologetically to the astonished general that he was just seeing how the thing worked.

Kennedy came to the Presidency during the years of the Cold War when our nuclear lead, and our aircraft carriers and armies standing all around the globe, were considered great international tranquilizers. National security was the biggest government concern when he entered the White House. His idea that we must change our strategic concepts and be prepared to fight "limited wars" in remote lands was basic to his opposition to Dulles's threat of "massive retaliation."

Personally, his most searing experience had been his command of *PT 109* and its destruction in the Pacific, his back injury, and the long road to recovery in the years that followed as he fought his way up the political ladder. On the walls of his office were pictures of ancient naval battles. There also hung the sword of John Barry, the Irish immigrant who was considered the father of the United States Navy.

Kennedy told Clifton in the early days that he wanted to visit representative units of all the armed forces. He wanted the men to know of his concern. He wanted to learn more about the state of the military as he went about the job of changing national military strategy. "What does a division look like?" he prodded Clifton. At Fort Bragg a whole division was drawn up to show him. He loved the demonstrations. Paratroops jumped in front of him. Special forces showed their prowess in judo and hand-to-hand combat, grunting, yelling, leaping, and falling. Kennedy's interest never faltered throughout the afternoon.

It was Kennedy who gave the Special Forces back their green berets, the World War II symbol of their kind of warfare. But Kennedy's belief in his Admirals and Generals was in no way total, particularly after the Bay of Pigs. He didn't blame them, really. He blamed himself. But he blamed himself for not questioning his military advisers more thoroughly and for not being as skeptical of their conclusions as of his advisors' judgments. Kennedy was distressed that his Air Force Chief Curtis LeMay did not fully understand the Air Force budget, but he made allowances. "When you go to war, you want LeMay in the leading bomber," he said one night. "But you don't want to ask him if you should go to war."

Military potential fascinated him, nonetheless. It was while he was aboard the *Enterprise* in the Atlantic in 1962 watching a naval fly-by that Secretary of Defense Robert McNamara leaned close and asked, "Why do they need all those different kinds of planes?" That was the birth of the TFX fighter, a plane which was born of noble concept but which never could meet the practical tests.

With Kennedy's Presidency came full use of the jet plane, *Air Force One*. It, too, played a role in changing that office. In the big, gleaming Boeing 707 a President could fly across the nation in a single day, sweeping down on half a dozen cities. He could then sleep in his bed aboard the plane as it roared back to Washington through the night. The President could be at his desk at the normal hour the next morning reasonably refreshed.

Kennedy loved the airplane, the feeling of movement, and the powerful impact it gave. He could pack almost the whole Oval Office on board and take off. He prepared for his meeting with Nikita Khrushchev in the cabin of *Air Force One* as he flew from Paris to Vienna. With the jet and the accompanying swarm of presidential helicopters he barnstormed Ireland in the summer of 1963, an emotional and joyous return to the "old sod" that may not have done much for international diplomacy, but which left everybody glowing who was touched by the tour. When he traveled he insisted that the full effectiveness of the office go along, most importantly, the trappings of communication. He insisted that the word to home be kept as clear as possible. All of his officers and aides should know where he was and what he was doing, so they could get their questions to him.

He insisted that everything be up to snuff—especially himself. Before his first European trip he injured his back in a tree planting ceremony in Canada. Yet, in Europe he refused to walk on crutches though his doctors recommended it. He simply wasn't going to meet Charles de Gaulle as a cripple, or confront Khrushchev on crutches, he told Clifton. He endured the pain.

Kennedy's White House was not an unrelieved vista of poise and good humor. There were emotional bottoms too. Perhaps he was lowest after the Bay of Pigs. Later that year when he had listened to the threats of Khrushchev, had watched the news accounts of the imposition of the Berlin Wall, gotten grim scientific reports on the tests of huge Soviet H bombs, he struggled against a deep despondency. His salvation was his understanding that events and moods change swiftly. There came the Nuclear Test-Ban Treaty and the Cuban missile triumph, the revival of the American economy, and his own growing sense of purpose.

In his last fall he traveled the length of the nation talking about environmental problems and extolling the end of nuclear atmospheric testing. It was, perhaps, the beginning of his presidential maturity. He knew the job, from Rose Garden to aircraft carrier. He had stood the test of the Soviets. There were faint flickers of progress in Congress. In his bearing and his words he showed just how glad he was to be President.

*The first head of state to make an official visit was Tunisia's Habib
Bourguiba, here viewing fireworks over the Washington Monument.*

Shortly after the inauguration former President Dwight Eisenhower returned to the White House. Ike told friends he was prepared to dislike young Kennedy, but in fact found him very charming.

On a New York visit to the United Nations, Kennedy meets with Ambassador Adlai Stevenson and Cambodia's Prince Norodom Sihanouk in the Carlyle Hotel, his headquarters in Manhattan.

PRECEDING SPREAD *Some twenty-five hundred high school students from fifty-six countries who had been living in the United States during the 1962–63 school year gathered in the Rose Garden. Their exuberance seen here prompted an amused Kennedy to say, "You are not the quietest group that has come to visit us at the White House." The President is in this picture.*

John Kennedy loved political campaigning. It was a relief from the White House routine and all his partisan juices could flow again. In St. Paul at the traditional bean dinner in 1962 he twitted his former Senate colleagues Hubert Humphrey and Eugene McCarthy. "It is worth coming fifteen hundred miles from Boston for a bean supper."

14

At the time of the Berlin Crisis in 1961, the entire 82nd Airborne Division (sixteen thousand men) was drawn up at Fort Bragg for the President's review.

Left, Brigadier General William P. Yarborough, Commander of Special Forces, thanks the President for giving back the "green berets," their symbol from World War II commando days.

Below, after Khrushchev threatened an age of global tension, Kennedy asked to see our newest weapons for guerrilla warfare. Here Clifton shows him the rifle for jungle warfare and an actual adaptation of the old crossbow.

Kennedy's favorite conference position in the Oval Office was his rocking chair in front of the fireplace. Here he meets with Secretary of Defense Robert McNamara and Secretary of State Dean Rusk.

The President and Mrs. Kennedy in a receiving line at the United Nations following his speech to the General Assembly in 1961. Israel's Golda Meir stands in front of the First Lady. Assembly President Mongi Slim, Tunisia, is at left.

OVERLEAF Kennedy speaks before the United Nations General Assembly. It was a time of international tension in Berlin and in Southeast Asia, a time, too, of sadness, following the death of UN Secretary General Dag Hammarskjold.

17

Kennedy's tour of Venezuela and Colombia in the fall of 1962 was a triumph. He was greeted by smiles and moving pleas for help for the poverty-stricken.

Kennedy greets team captains in the annual all-star game in 1963. Left to right, House Speaker John McCormack, Vice-President Lyndon Johnson, aide Dave Powers (the in-house baseball

expert), Senator Hubert Humphrey, the President, Commissioner Ford Frick, American League's Luis Aparicio, the National League's Stan Musial, Secret Service Agent Jerry Behn.

Kennedy understood the working men of the press better than any modern President. He knew their deadlines, special needs and prejudices, and most of their editors. He was quick with compliments for work he liked, even quicker with his irritation over critical articles and newscasts. He often stopped reporters for quick conferences in the midst of his duties, as with Sidey, below, following an Oval Office speech on the economy. Right, his press conferences in the State Department auditorium were called "the best matinee" in town. Kennedy pioneered the use of television, kept himself open for interviews, as with Walter Cronkite at Hyannisport at the summer White House on Squaw Island.

Congressional leaders take time out from a strategy breakfast with Kennedy to watch the blast-off of Astronaut John Glenn, February 21, 1962. Left, Kennedy and Glenn at Cape Canaveral inspect the capsule. In the Rose Garden Kennedy awards the NASA Distinguished Service Medal to Astronaut L. Gordon Cooper.

A moment of triumph. Kennedy prepares to sign the Nuclear

Test-Ban Treaty in the old Treaty Room in the mansion.

PRECEDING SPREAD *The climax of the thirteen days of the Cuban Missile Crisis in October 1962. Members of the National Security Council's Executive Committee (ExComm) meet in the Cabinet Room framing U.S. answers to Khrushchev as events began to go our way. At the heart of Kennedy's strategy was his insistence to leave the Soviets a way out. "There is nothing more dangerous than a cornered bear." Left, standing, Attorney General Robert Kennedy. Clockwise at the table from left, Assistant Secretary of Defense Paul Nitze, Deputy USIA Director Donald Wilson, Special Counsel Theodore Sorensen, Executive Secretary NSC Bromley Smith, Special Assistant McGeorge Bundy, Secretary of the Treasury Douglas Dillon, Vice-President Johnson, Ambassador Llewellyn Thompson, William C. Foster, CIA Director John McCone (hidden), the President, Secretary of State Dean Rusk, Secretary of Defense Robert McNamara, Deputy Secretary of Defense Roswell Gilpatric, Chairman JCS, Maxwell Taylor.*

Above, one of the small, silver calendars outlining the thirteen crucial days of the Missile Crisis. Kennedy had thirty of them made by Tiffany's and gave them to his key people. The initials of the recipients were in the left corner. This one was given to Jackie Kennedy. Right, the crisis was marked with small, somber huddles like this one on the porch outside the President's office. Left to right, Bundy, the President, Taylor, McNamara.

Yugoslavia's President Marshal Josip Broz Tito stands with Kennedy during official welcoming ceremonies on the South Lawn in October 1963. The Tito visit was one part of Kennedy's effort to reduce tension between the U.S. and the Communist world, a hope he had held out in his American University speech the spring before.

In 1962 Kennedy meets with Russians in the Oval Office. Left to right, Vladimir Semenor, Deputy Minister of Foreign Affairs, Ambassador Anatoly Dobrynin, and Andrei Gromyko, Minister of Foreign Affairs.

Kennedy at a university ceremony in a robe with his mortarboard in his lap. Here, at Vanderbilt University, he gave an address urging, in the words of Aristotle, "It is they who act who rightly win the prizes."

OVERLEAF *The climax of Kennedy's 1963 trip to Europe. In front of West Berlin's City Hall before nearly a million cheering Germans, Kennedy delivered his memorable line, "Today, in the world of freedom, the proudest boast is 'Ich bin ein Berliner.'"*

The key Kennedy pressed to open the Seattle World's Fair in April 1962 had been used by seven Presidents in such historic ceremonies as the opening of the Panama Canal. This time radio waves from the star Cassiopeia A were used to activate the machinery, an illustration of the space-age theme of the fair.

A minor achievement in Kennedy's 1963 tour of Germany was bringing West Berlin's Mayor Willy Brandt and German Chancellor Konrad Adenauer together publicly, shown here in Kennedy's limousine.

Italy was the last stop on Kennedy's foreign tour in 1963. In Rome he told his audience, "I represent two or three times as many Americans of Italian descent as the Mayor does."

In England on the same journey, Kennedy went to Prime Minister
Harold MacMillan's country home, Birch Grove, Sussex, for brief talks.

In Ireland during his 1963 trip, Kennedy was cheered every step of the way. He almost always stopped to greet his well-wishers.

Princess Beatrix of the Netherlands gets a first-hand look at the Dutch tulips, of which Kennedy was immensely proud, in the Rose Garden on her visit to Washington in 1963.

Germany's Chancellor Konrad Adenauer shows his skill as a grandfather scooping up John-John during a 1962 visit to Washington. A copy of this picture was given to Adenauer and he was so taken with it he sent Stoughton an inscribed pictorial biography of himself.

*The President and Vice-President Lyndon B. Johnson stroll down the
drive on the South Lawn. An unusual view of the two by themselves.*

Two men expected to be opposing presidential candidates. Here Kennedy grips Senator Barry Goldwater's arm at the Rose Garden ceremony honoring retiring Air Force General Emmett (Rosie) O'Donnell, seen in center, background.

In the fall of 1963 Kennedy flew across the country to inspect natural resources and talk about conservation. But true to his political heritage, he mixed in some talk about the Nuclear Test-Ban Treaty. He received an enthusiastic response from this crowd in Montana.

Fenceside duty was something Kennedy relished, even when it meant sticking a few fingers through the fence links as on this trip to San Diego in 1963.

"I first of all want to express my appreciation to my brother Teddy for his offering me his coattail," quipped Kennedy. At the 1963 New England Salute to the President in Boston, Kennedy was on home ground with people he knew and loved.

OVERLEAF *Roadside audiences formed a whole area of study. On this California visit in 1963 Kennedy gets top rating with all generations.*

One of the most historic pictures in Stoughton's collection. This was taken at Hyde Park in November 1962 at the funeral of Eleanor Roosevelt. It includes one President, two former Presidents, and a President-to-be.

Special meeting in Kennedy's Hyannisport living room in 1961 on defense-scientific budget matters. Clockwise from left, Chairman of the Joint Chiefs Lyman L. Lemnitzer, Special Military Assistant Maxwell Taylor, Secretary of Defense Robert McNamara, the President, Director of the Budget David Bell, Deputy Secretary of Defense Roswell Gilpatric, and Scientific Adviser Jerome Weisner.

A commuting President waits for his helicopter. Kennedy catches up on his newspaper while the chopper settles into place on the South Lawn of the White House.

"One of the toughest jobs is to smile all day in a foreign language." ...JFK

When the Kennedys arrived at the White House, the kings and queens and prime ministers who came to Washington customarily were greeted on the barren tarmac of National Airport. The view was of hangars and oil spots. Commercial air traffic had to be halted for half an hour while honors were rendered, greetings exchanged. Occasionally, a pilot would not have gotten the word and the roar of engines would drown out the President and his guest.

Jackie Kennedy had a better idea. The ceremonies were moved to the South Lawn of the White House where the view of the Washington Monument and the Jefferson Memorial was spectacular, where the bands could play and not be overwhelmed by traffic noises, and where the President could take his visitors immediately inside and begin work. Thus it was that official pageantry was upgraded.

Our pageants have most often had a home-made look—Fourth of July parades with bicycles and horses and pretty girls on floats. The settings of our early history have been rather modest—Independence Hall and the White House. We have gloried not in kings and queens or even prime ministers and princes, but instead in the common man, and we have celebrated his small deeds in casual rituals.

In the early days of our history when whole counties would gather for political picnics in open meadows beside clear streams, the natural beauty was majesty enough. There was quiet and time was not short and people could linger and talk, creating a sense of national unity. In that time the White House and the Presidency were far away in every respect, not so central in everyone's life. There were then grander events in other cities than there were in the White House in Washington, D.C.

But in 1961 that changed. What made the difference was the use of the White House as a setting for the pageantry of the Presidency, an important, indeed, necessary part of governing in the new era of TV. "Thanks for the use of your house," Kennedy often joked to his audiences.

Kennedy's personal arena was the Rose Garden and it was redesigned to fit his needs. Since there was call almost every week for some small ceremonies just outside his office doors, he had special steps put in from which he could award medals, give talks to visiting 4-H clubs, and thank departing civil servants. It all was designed to get the maximum out of the natural beauty in the garden.

Shakespeare came to the East Room on a specially designed and constructed mini-stage that could be put up and collapsed with little effort. There was ballet, too, and chamber music, some of it not always to the liking of the President, who preferred light opera and semiclassical music, but he went along with Jackie, and always took a special pride in her taste.

In addition to the White House, Jackie decided to use another national monument in her entertaining. She had been profoundly impressed during her first official visit to Europe with the way the French used the splendor of Versailles to impress visitors. She brought the idea back home. To show their special thanks to Pakistan's President Ayub Khan, who had supported the U.S. policy in Laos, Jackie staged a State dinner for him on the lawn of Mount Vernon. The mosquitoes had to be dispelled with the help of the Army Engineers who sprayed four times before the dinner. And the indomitable Chef René Verdon figured out how to transport the food the several miles and still serve it hot. The guests were taken down the Potomac River on four Navy boats and whisked by limousine to the top of the hill where the Colonial Fife and Drum Corps in revolutionary uniforms showed close order drill as it had been performed for General George Washington. The dinner was on the lawn under a huge tent and the guests watched the light fade over the river. Then the National Symphony played under the massive old elm trees, the imposing façade of Mount Vernon floodlighted in the background. This was something new in American pageantry.

The great cellist Pablo Casals, in self-imposed exile in Puerto Rico for twenty years, returned to play at a White House dinner for Puerto Rico's Governor Muñoz Marin and in special tribute to the Kennedys. All the Nobel Prize winners from the Western Hemisphere were invited to another even more spectacular dinner. But probably the most elegance was shown when France's Minister of Culture André Malraux came to visit and Jackie showed her special thanks to him for the courtesies he had lavished on her in Paris in 1961.

For Cecil Stoughton the moments of pageantry were naturals. The people were famous, the settings superb. He had only to unlimber his camera and shoot to record significant vignettes of history. But Jackie Kennedy did not like the events to be disrupted by flashing strobe units. Stoughton was asked to be as discreet as he could be, to fade into the walls and take his pictures by natural light, and then move out quickly. He was hardly noticed, but he never missed an evening. He was on the South Lawn in the cool night air to catch the reflection of the fireworks that burst over the Washington Monument in celebration of the dinner for Tunisia's Habib Bourguiba. He knelt silently to squeeze off the frames of Pablo Casals playing in the East Room.

For Ted Clifton the afternoons and evenings of pageantry were busy times. He was a logistics maestro of sorts, a personal message-bearer, a man who in various ways helped the social secretaries make sure things went off on schedule. He had been a part of military pomp for years, but the Kennedy White House was new to him too. No detail, he soon learned, was left to chance. Nothing was to be done in mediocre fashion.

The President had a fetish about the wines which were to be served. Although he was not a noted connoisseur, he knew that others were. Before a state dinner he took it upon himself to sample the vintages. Clifton would see him around 6 P.M. stopping off at the dining room to taste the wines—one was often an American product, a second from the country of the guest when possible, the third inevitably a French wine.

Kennedy fretted about the fact that he had no adequate medal to give special foreigners and distinguished Americans to show appreciation for their support and friendship. The only medal which he could by law award was the Medal of Freedom, a tiny bronze medallion which had little meaning since it was passed out by the hundreds during World War II to American civilians who contributed to the war effort. "Let's invent a medal," he told Clifton. "But don't make it like the Queen's Honors list." He didn't want to be put in the inflexible position of having to produce a list each year. The political pressure brought to bear for such awards could be intolerable.

Under Clifton's guidance the Freedom Medal was redesigned into a handsome silver and enamel medallion, with accompanying blue ribbons bedecked with the Federal eagle. A committee was appointed and a special list of outstanding Americans was drawn up and Kennedy had his day with a White House reception for this collection of men and women who had done something special for America.

The Kennedys found the graceful dome of the Jefferson Memorial a disappointment at night because it was not floodlighted. At their request, Clifton and the Army found some old searchlights and bathed the monument in their intense candle power. The trees of the South Lawn were trimmed to give an unob-structed view of the new spectacle, which later was made permanent. Kennedy also complained about the temporary buildings still squatting on the Mall from World Wars I and II. He wanted them torn down and the natural beauty of the Mall restored. The ideas for the restoration of Lafayette Park and the improvement of Pennsylvania Avenue took root in these years as well.

In most ceremonial matters the President and Jackie came to easy agreement no matter how they started out. But now and then there were unexpected differences. In such cases, Jackie usually won. Clifton remembers the night that Kennedy summoned him to his table in the State Dining Room and muttered a mild complaint about the music the Marine Band was playing. "Let's get something livelier," he said. As Clifton set off to complete the mission, good judgment overwhelmed him. He went to Jackie, who was presiding at the head table in the Blue Room, and he relayed the President's request. "Oh, he does?" she said, surprised. "What does he suggest?" Clifton said the President had in mind some semiclassical numbers. Jackie gave Clifton her most innocent look. "I chose that music myself. But, if he insists, have them play 'Hail to the Chief' over and over. That should amuse him." Clifton abandoned the mission.

Special mementos for the visitors were another concern during state occasions. Albums of photos of the visits were big hits. The prints were rushed through in a few hours so the visitors could see themselves, almost while their performances were still going on. Both the President and Jackie concerned themselves with the official gifts which protocol demanded they exchange with visitors. They looked for books, gemstones, and paintings, things that told the history of the United States.

When Kennedy received a glittering sword from the King of Morocco he queried Clifton as to whether such a gift could be fashioned from anything in America's past. The sword George Washington carried into battle was among the Smithsonian exhibits and the President concurred with Clifton that skillful replicas would make handsome presents. Clifton went to the Rock Island arsenal for help. They searched out old craftsmen who used to fashion cavalry saber blades to turn out the new swords. The ivory in the handle of the Washington weapon was an exotic green which Clifton found he had to go to the chemical experts of the Dupont company to get reproduced precisely. The final products were so perfect that they were sent to the Smithsonian to be marked so that they would never be mistaken for the real thing. John Kennedy decreed that they would be given to special guests at special times. And one was set aside for his son.

One of the most eloquent and significant evenings at the White House was this dinner in April 1962 given for Nobel Prize winners of the Western Hemisphere. "I think this is the most extraordinary collection of talent, of human knowledge, that has ever been gathered together at the White House, with the possible exception of when Thomas Jefferson dined alone," said Kennedy.

Another memorable White House dinner was given for Puerto Rico's Governor Muñoz Marin in November 1961. Cellist Pablo Casals broke a long exile from the United States out of respect for Kennedy and Marin. Here Kennedy congratulates the artist following his performance.

At the Nobel dinner, Author Pearl Buck talks with Kennedy while Poet Robert Frost is entertained by Jackie.

Right, the President and Mrs. Kennedy at the close of a white tie evening honoring the Grand Duchess Charlotte and Prince Jean of Luxembourg. Kennedy seemed to enjoy these evenings more than he admitted.

Trooping the line of the ceremonial honor guard became a part of the pageantry of the South Lawn. Official welcomes had become too noisy and inconvenient at Washington's National Airport.

Jackie and Caroline received a gift from Pakistan's President Ayub Khan—Sardar, a well-trained gelding. This was thanks for Jackie's visit to Pakistan in 1962. A groom makes the presentation at Fort Myer. Part of Arlington National Cemetery is in the background.

Left, members of Great Britain's famed Black Watch Regiment perform on the South Lawn in November 1963. The kilted Scottish pipers and drill team represented a unit which had fought all over the world, including action against the colonies in the Revolutionary War. Caroline hugs her father while John-John turns to inspect the shako of the Black Watch Commander.

Below, like millions of other U. S. tourists, Kennedy pauses during his 1962 trip to Independence Hall, Philadelphia, to touch the Liberty Bell. His speech that day "stressed [in honoring the Constitution] not only independence but interdependence—not the individual liberty of one but the indivisible liberty of all."

Below, a familiar scene at the bottom of the stairs in the White House foyer on formal nights. The President and Mrs. Kennedy, the former President and Mrs. Truman receive honors as they prepare to go to dinner. Behind them, left to right, General Clifton, the Clifton Daniels, and Naval Aide Tazewell Shepard.

In November 1961 the Kennedys gave a dinner for the Trumans. Highlight of the evening was when Truman himself sat down at the piano in the East Room to thump out his theme song, "The Missouri Waltz." Standing behind him is Eugene List, the evening's performer, who had played for Truman at Potsdam in 1945, when List was a staff sergeant, and Truman was making final peace plans with Churchill and Stalin.

Kennedy paid his respects to the American war dead on Veterans' Day, November 11, 1963, at Arlington National Cemetery. Right, he stands in silence as taps are sounded at the Tomb of the Unknown Soldiers. That day, he brought John-John to see the ceremony. Below, the young boy imitates his father as he marches up the drive to meet him.

During his 1963 Dublin visit, Kennedy stands in silence at

Arbour Hill before the graves of the heroes of the 1916 uprising.

Dinner on the lawn of Mount Vernon in 1961 for Pakistan's President Ayub Khan. Above, the Colonial Fife and Drum Corps performs on the green in front of George Washington's mansion before the dinner. Stoughton took this picture from the house's cupola. Right, Jackie presides over her table beside Ayub (on her right). Vice-President Johnson is at right.

Great Britain's Prime Minister Harold MacMillan and Kennedy met frequently during these years. Most of their meetings were informal, working sessions. Kennedy gives his welcome speech at this arrival in April 1962 at Andrews Air Force Base.

OVERLEAF *One of the most colorful cavalcades of his Presidency was this greeting for Kennedy in Mexico City. Clouds of large red, white, and blue confetti literally filled the air, sometimes obscuring the view.*

Kennedy strides onto the red carpet in Mexico in June 1962 for a warm clasp from President Adolfo Lopez Mateos. At first Kennedy declined the traditional abrazo *and devised this "limited edition."*

"I am the man who accompanied Jacqueline Kennedy to Paris, and I have enjoyed it." ... JFK

They came from the relative privacy of Georgetown where friends could be chosen with care and the public walled away with ease. While John Kennedy had a portion of the rollicking Irishman in him, Jackie Kennedy never did. She needed privacy for nourishment.

The roaring crowds of the campaign trail held a certain fascination for her. But she soon tired of them, and sought out the quiet of her own parlor. She was intrigued by the men of power, but in limited numbers. She really preferred to watch the game through a window.

In fact, the President probably was the most withdrawn of the men in his family, finding deep satisfaction in hours of reading and quiet talk. But his adult life had been a public life and the exposure did not hold that many horrors for him.

The contrast between this man and wife was no more profound, however, than that between many men and women who live together happily. These two lived in growing harmony in the White House. Clifton and Stoughton, did, by the nature of their duties, see them enough to conclude that stories of dissent and conflict were untrue. Disagreements were resolved in a civilized fashion. There were impositions on their time that sometimes brought irritation to one or both but those moments passed, too. In the curious manner of the White House, while being pulled apart in many official ways, the two were moved closer together by the massive public scrutiny.

The early months were hardest on Jackie. She once described the White House as being something like a hotel. Every time she looked down a corridor, there was some strange person guarding the door or shuttling into the President's bedroom with a message. She defied the system at times with considerable imagination and daring. But her eloquence and sense of history was so impressive that her "differentness" simply strengthened the public's fascination with her.

Her image with some was one of a slender butterfly flitting through the corridors of power, her only visible duty to look and act a part. She did that; but, further, Jackie was probably first and foremost a mother and a wife. She was fiercely protective of the world which she created for her children and her husband within the White House. It was filled with small, unrecorded rituals of special meaning. She brought the children to their father at times when it meant the most to him. She planned recreation for the President to give him needed interludes in the daily grind. There were quiet weekend dinners with friends and family. Now and then there was a private dinner dance for their old Georgetown friends and out-of-town acquaintances. "It was the gayest, most magnificent party I've ever attended," said columnist Rowland Evans, Jr., after the first of such affairs.

It was Jackie who scheduled the movies. She suggested a swimming party in the redecorated White House pool. She came around to the Oval Office in sweater and jodhpurs looking young and alive, a proud President introduced her to his guest, who was taken by the casualness. She was the one who enlisted Stoughton to put on film the record of the family in the White House. Jackie wanted the best food she could serve and found a chef who could cook it.

There was no kitchen on the third floor of the White House and the Kennedys soon found that it was a chore to bring the food for their family all the way from the basement. She had a kitchen installed, not only for convenience and efficiency, but also so there would be a place the family could gather for a snack when they didn't want the official staff intruding into their lives. In every President's White House there is a quiet struggle to find moments and places of total privacy.

In their search for privacy and a family life, they were never unmindful of the demands being made on the numerous staff members. Each person who worked with them can recount a time when Jackie or the President were especially thoughtful. One night when Jackie had planned a movie at Hammersmith Farm, her home in Newport, Rhode Island, Stoughton was setting up the gear. "Do you have a family," she asked Stoughton. When he said that he did, she replied, "Why don't you go home this weekend and be with them? There is nothing special here." Stoughton mumbled something about working for the President. Jackie turned to her husband, "Why can't Captain

Stoughton go home and be with his family?" The President look blank. "I don't know, why not?" So it was. That weekend the Captain went home to be with his family.

Despite the constant entreaties of the photographers, the President was never seen to kiss his wife in public. Such displays of affection before cameras he considered to be in bad taste. His feelings were not hidden, however, when Jackie was taken to the hospital in Hyannisport in 1963 for the premature birth of Patrick, who died two days later. Kennedy, in Washington, dropped everything he was doing and sped to her side in the first Air Force plane he could find (his own plane was off on a training mission).

His pride in his wife's achievements was monumental. She spoke in French with Charles de Gaulle in 1961, and Kennedy told the world he was the man who had come to Paris with Jacqueline Kennedy. He stood beside her and beamed when she spoke to the Bay of Pigs veterans in Spanish and again when she did the same thing for Mexican-Americans in Houston.

Sometimes he had to bargain with her for her help, but that was done in good humor. Once there was a question as to whether she would show up for a Girl Scout ceremony in the Rose Garden. Kennedy talked it over with her, then came back to the Oval Office and told Pierre Salinger that she had agreed to do it. Salinger gave the President a skeptical look. "Okay," answered Kennedy, "I traded a symphony and a ballet for it, but she will be there."

Maybe it was during the Cuban Missile Crisis when husband and wife meant the most to each other. At night after the long hours of secret planning Kennedy would walk alone on the grounds of the White House trying to clear his mind. Jackie would walk out to meet him and the two would go back inside for dinner where he would tell her everything that was happening. When Kennedy gave his key men silver calendars with the thirteen crucial days of October marked off, he made a special point of giving one to Jackie too.

Kennedy speaks to the press informally in front of the entrance to the West Wing of the White House.

OVERLEAF *On the night of November 21, 1963, the Kennedys were in Houston campaigning. Appearing before the League of United Latin American Citizens, Kennedy spoke in English and introduced Jackie, "In order that my words will be even clearer, I am going to ask my wife to say a few words to you also." Jackie spoke Spanish much to the delight of the crowd and her husband.*

The President's forty-sixth birthday on May 29, 1963, was a brief interlude of fun and games and a muted show of affection, the way Kennedy liked it. At right, in the morning he found in his office a bouquet of forty-six red roses. He posed stiffly for Stoughton, like an Irish alderman. Later, the staff held a surprise party in the White House mess. Above, Kennedy reads the card on a special basket of crab grass from the Rose Garden.

Right, the President and his wife wait at Union Station in October 1963 for the arrival of Ethiopia's King Haile Selassie, who had decided to travel by train from New York.

Jackie Kennedy in July 1963 looks out over the ocean off Cape Cod. These moments on board the Honey Fitz *were the most relaxed for both Kennedys. They were away from the phone and for the most part the prying eyes of the press and the public.*

Two studies of the First Couple. The picture at left was taken in the Oval Office following an informal ceremony. At right, they listen to the remarks of the Commander of the Black Watch on the South Lawn.

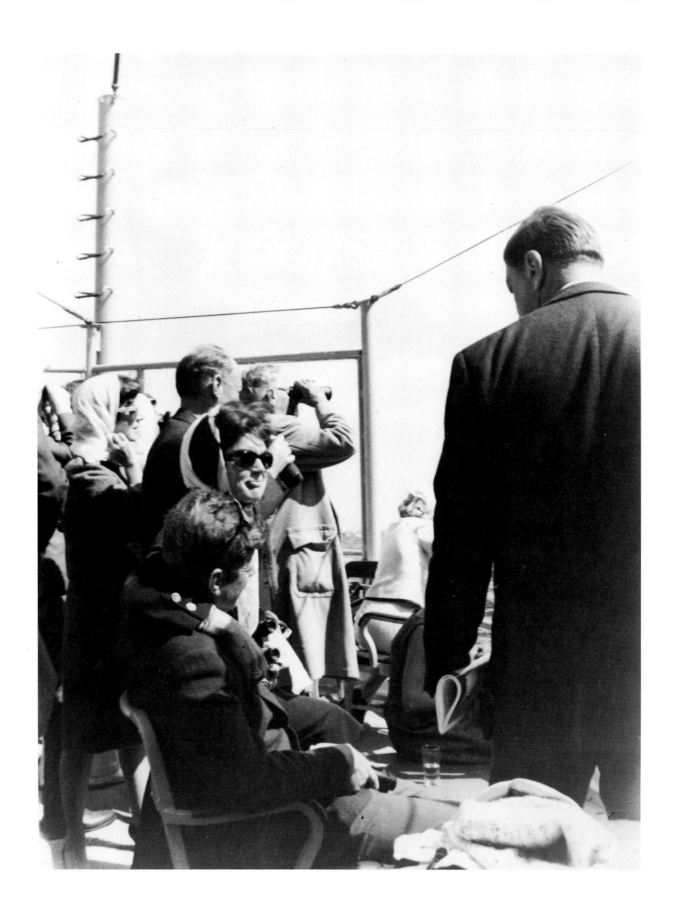

The First Couple aboard the destroyer USS *Joseph P. Kennedy, Jr., watching the America's Cup yacht races off Newport in 1962. It was the kind of day they liked—pageantry mixed with friends and sunshine and sea.*

Jackie makes a special point with the President at the dinner given by the Australian Ambassador Sir Howard Beale for the crews of the two boats. The dinner was held in The Breakers, the legendary mansion in Newport built by Cornelius Vanderbilt, and now a historic monument.

*Below, First Couple emerge from the District of Columbia
Armory after a special gala saluting Kennedy in 1962.*

The Kennedys made a point of greeting and thanking entertainers who came to White House dinners to perform in the East Room. Here, their pleasure at what they had just seen, is obvious.

Right, Jackie, in informal riding attire, shows the President two marble plaques received from Italian craftsmen, presented by Prime Minister Amintore Fanfani.

Left, Military Aide Clifton hears from President Kennedy what he did not like about welcoming ceremonies for dignitaries at National Airport. Jackie listens in amusement. Though he seldom wore one, Kennedy dutifully carried a hat to support the industry.

The President (left) watches his wife ride Sardar over their farm, Wexford, at Atoka, Virginia, the weekend before their Dallas trip in 1963. Jackie had organized a small horse show among friends and neighbors for that day, but heavy rains prevented the horse vans from coming to Atoka. Jackie and Caroline were the main performers.

November 22, 1963. In Fort Worth, Texas, as he prepares to go on to Dallas, Kennedy speaks to a political rally in a hotel parking lot. Jackie did not come down for the early morning meeting. Here, Kennedy points to their hotel room, saying, "Mrs. Kennedy is organizing herself. It takes longer, but, of course, she looks better than we do when she does it."

Reviewing the veterans of the Bay of Pigs in Miami in December 1962, Jackie gave her speech in Spanish. Her short talk on their courage was the hit of the day. Here, she greets some of the veterans at the close of the ceremony.

"*If I knew the secret of this family, I would bottle it and sell it.*" ... Joseph Kennedy

One night a few days before John Kennedy became President his father talked about the family. The patriarch sat in his modest office on New York's Park Avenue, worrying about his inaugural dress and wondering aloud what now would happen in his tightly knit family. "Jack doesn't belong any more to just a family," he said. "He belongs to the country. That's probably the saddest thing about all this. The family can be there. But there is not much they can do sometimes for the President of the United States."

In fact, Joe Kennedy was only half right. John Kennedy did belong to the country. But he never abandoned his family. And in some way, the members became even closer. Joe Kennedy had unknowingly explained that, too. He had told his sons, he once mused, that as they went through life they would be most fortunate if they could number true friends on one hand. Therefore, he counseled them, stay close to your own family.

Bobby Kennedy became Attorney General after some hesitation and a good deal of family joking about on-the-job training. Brother-in-law R. Sargent Shriver took responsibility for the Peace Corps and Stephen Smith, another brother-in-law, helped out in the White House for a time. Teddy Kennedy's interest in politics grew until he decided to run for the President's old Senate seat when it was up again, and he won. Nor was the father ignored. Joe Kennedy imposed an arms-length relationship with the White House, knowing how much some of his old business antagonists would criticize if he seemed to be giving too much advice. But the President called his father, both before and after his stroke, almost every night to bring him up to date on what was going on in the Oval Office and to chat about family matters as well.

Family life swirled around the patriarch even when he was confined to a wheelchair. He was out on the porch of the Hyannisport home for almost every arrival and departure of the President. He was ribbed at family parties as in the old days. And even though he could not talk, he was talked to as if nothing had happened. When the children came by the Oval Office in their Halloween costumes one year, Stoughton recalls, the President was so amused that he immediately picked up the phone and had the White House switchboard get Joe Kennedy in Hyannisport so the young goblins could try a trick or treat line on "Grandpa."

In the three White House years Bobby Kennedy became even closer to his older brother. He was a counselor on almost all matters. Bobby considered his only task was to help the President succeed. Having no concerns about money, freed of personal political ambition for the time being, he could be candid with his brother when others hesitated. He could be daring when others were timid. He became almost a part of the White House staff.

One visitor remembers talking to the President in front of the fireplace in the Oval Office when the door to the garden suddenly burst open and in stalked Bobby Kennedy, hands in his pockets. The President simply glanced that way, said nothing, turned back to his guest. Bobby said nothing, walked straight through the office and out the other door just as if he took that kind of a short cut every day, and maybe he did. The sisters—Eunice Shriver, Jean Smith, and Pat Lawford—helped too, sometimes being hostesses when Jackie was unavailable. Rose Kennedy was a substitute hostess also.

When together the Kennedy family members did their best to top each other with humor. Perhaps they tried too much sometimes, but it was a family touched with tragedy even then and they had long ago decided that life while it lasted should have laughter.

Back from his second European trip, Kennedy was eager to see the movies which Stoughton had made and, since his sisters had traveled with him, he eyed the rerun of their performances with special interest. He roared with laughter when the film revealed that Jean Smith and sister-in-law Lee Radziwill had turned up in Great Britain wearing identical white coats. One picture showed their backs as they stood side by side, sister Jean's coat longer than sister-in-law Lee's. Kennedy had the movie stopped to study the scene. Perfect, he decided, for a family gag. He had Stoughton make a life-sized blowup of that particular frame and swore him to secrecy. Then, the next time that the family gathered, Kennedy had Stoughton suddenly thrust the huge picture through a door. The gag brought the house down.

An annual family ritual was the Labor Day softball game against the rest of the Hyannisport neighborhood. It was played on the field in front of the main house, which Joe Kennedy had purchased just for such contests. Kennedy's back was too tender for him to participate during his White House years. But he sat on the bench and coached. One year he arranged for two top-notch players from Otis Air Force Base to be brought over and mixed in the family team as if they were relatives or friends. The President thoroughly enjoyed watching these two ringers clout hit after hit and win a smashing victory over the opposing neighborhood team. Then he confessed.

One afternoon Kennedy rode out on the *Honey Fitz* to watch Teddy compete in one of the big regattas. From the start Kennedy was aghast at his brother's mistakes. He shouted to Stoughton to take pictures of the race. When the film was developed the President had a delightful evening showing Teddy all his sailing mistakes.

The matter of friends was more difficult than family. The old friends of Kennedy's had their own families, had careers to pursue. It was not always easy to get them together. Red Fay, a friend from the President's Navy days, came back from California and took a job as Under Secretary of the Navy. The two couples shared many pleasant evenings after the nation's business had been finished. Congressman Torbert McDonald, a Harvard friend, was nearby, and other friends from the Hill such as George Smathers came by. But the casual relationships of earlier days were of necessity curtailed. Every word the President said, everything he did was material for Washington gossip. And Kennedy, being an irreverent man, could make remarks about events and people which made superb reading.

For the most part, Kennedy clung to his eldest and truest friends from boyhood and college. Lem Billings and Chuck Spaulding were around the White House constantly, sacrificing their personal ambitions for this friendship and their own fascination at being near the center of power.

Kennedy's journalistic compatriots were yet another part of his personal world. Some of them like columnist Charles Bartlett were long-time friends. The President and Jackie had met at dinner at the Bartlett's house. Ben Bradlee and his wife Toni had been Georgetown neighbors of the Kennedys and had come to be close friends that way and also through Ben's work as *Newsweek*'s bureau chief, then Washington *Post* editor. These friends traveled a difficult course sometimes. They had great affection for Kennedy and enjoyed his company immensely. They also had their jobs to do. Since Kennedy was the biggest story in Washington they often found themselves participating in presidential events as friends, then being called on to write about them as journalists. For the most part there was no strain. While such friends sometimes let private views of the President and Jackie slip into print, Kennedy understood their problem of divided loyalty. For every Bartlett or Bradlee there were twenty-five other Washington journalists who had known Kennedy quite well on the Hill and he continued to count them all as special people.

However, the general problem of friendships for a President bothered Kennedy some. He once mentioned the difficulties a President had in making new friends. It did not take long for his sensitive political antennae to detect what the proximity of such vast power did to ambitious or greedy people. He could see through overly eager professions of loyalty and sudden changes in political philosophy by those on the make in Washington. While Kennedy gathered new people around him professionally and made many fast friends in that way, for instance, Robert McNamara, he did not venture beyond this proving ground for companionship.

When Joe Kennedy could no longer preside over his family the job was taken over by John Kennedy. He was the eldest son. It was that simple. And there were times when taking care of the family came first. When a request from the United States embassy in London came through the State Department for a portrait of ex-Ambassador Joe Kennedy, it was sent on to the President. He never thought of delegating such a matter. He muttered something to himself about having to call all the family members and get some money from each of them because none would want to be left out. Then call he did—each one. He carefully explained the project, asked for the donation, and completed the transaction. It never seemed to occur to John Kennedy that he could push all this aside since, as his father said, he really belonged to the country. But perhaps because he stayed so much a family man was one reason the country liked him so well.

OVERLEAF *In this 1962 family birthday present for Joseph P. Kennedy, Stoughton created a montage showing all the sons and daughters and all the grandchildren. The montage is made of four separate pictures—a master picture of most of the family members in front of the family house in Hyannisport, a picture of Teddy Kennedy and his two children taken at his Cape home, a picture of Stephen Smith and his family taken at yet another place in Hyannisport, and a final shot of Peter Lawford taken at Malibu Beach.*

One of the more memorable pictures of John and Robert Kennedy together. Stoughton snapped this in the Rose Garden, when the Attorney General presented the recipients of the Young American Medals to the President, who then awarded the medals.

The President with his mother, Rose Kennedy, at the First International Awards Dinner of the Joseph P. Kennedy, Jr. Foundation held at Washington's Statler-Hilton in 1962.

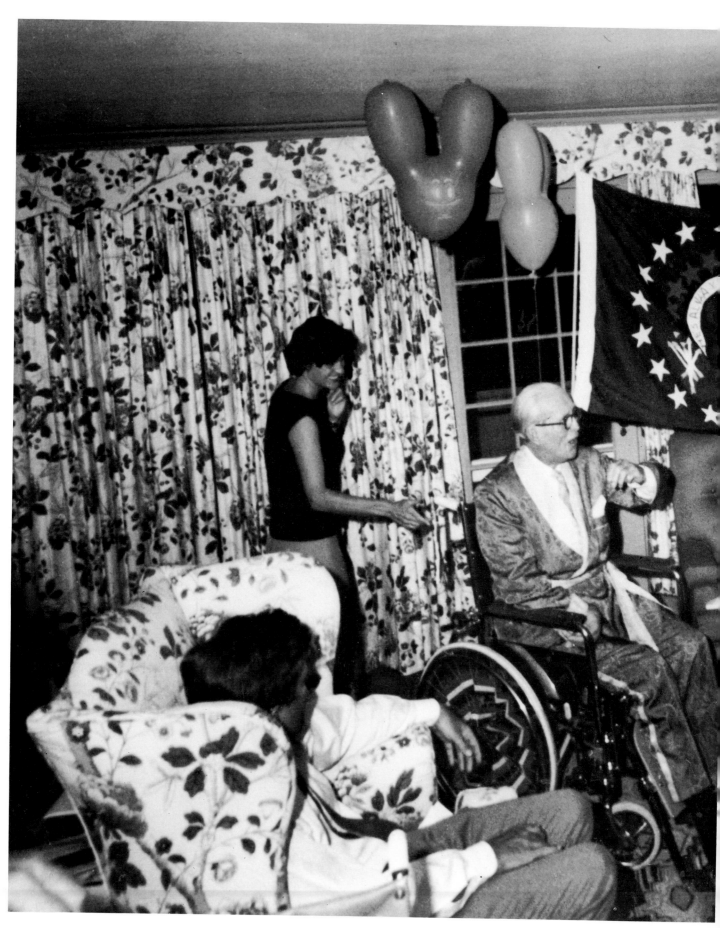

The celebration of Joseph P. Kennedy's seventy-fifth birthday at the Cape. Here, family members go through traditional jokes and teasing. For this party in 1963 there were skits, song parodies, and, of course, a cake. The President watches from a chair in foreground. Left of the elder Kennedy is Ann Gargan, his niece. Others visible, left to right, Sargent Shriver, Pat Lawford, and Bobby Kennedy.

Kennedy visits with relatives on the old sod in Duganstown, Ireland, during his visit in the summer of 1963. Kennedy's grandfather, Patrick Kennedy, spent his early years on this farm. To the right of Kennedy is his cousin Mrs. Mary Ryan who assembled twenty-five relatives and the parish priest for the reunion.

112

Bobby Kennedy and five of his children in front of his father's home on the Cape.

One of the few times that Stoughton asked the President for a specific picture. Learning that the brothers were all together, he told Kennedy he did not have a shot of the three of them in the White House. The President liked the idea too, summoned Bobby from his limousine, and guided Teddy to the Rose Garden porch where they posed in high spirits, Bobby bending his knees to emphasize that he was the smallest.

"Keep shooting Captain, you are about to see a President eaten by a horse." . . . JFK

There are those who insist that John Kennedy was always relaxed. They never saw him in a long and anxious hour of crisis. Yet, even in those times Kennedy introduced small moments of relief. In the midst of the Cuban Missile Crisis, when a U-2 flying from Alaska lost its bearings and the plane headed over the Soviet Union, Kennedy said wryly, "There is always some S.O.B. who doesn't get the word."

Secretary of Defense Robert McNamara recalls that Kennedy could always produce a phrase that would restore perspective, could by tone of voice re-establish reality and ultimate confidence. In a sense, tension never ruled the Kennedy White House.

There was another side to that coin, however. No matter how far from the White House, the President was on the job. What evolved in the end was a running drama of work and play, of laughter in the midst of substance, of work intruding while Kennedy sailed the sunlit seas off Hyannisport. It all seemed to fit naturally into the Kennedy Presidency.

He and Jackie had their special likes, of course. The ultimate afternoon was the President seated in his special leather swivel chair in the stern of the *Honey Fitz* cruising the familiar Cape Cod waters with his family around him. He perused the newspapers with a special relish on these days, catching up on the human events in the nation that sometimes he had to brush by during his workdays. He wore sports shirts and liked a cigar or two after he had dined on his favorite fish chowder. It was best when the children were there with their puppies or friends or both. The President always liked some of his friends aboard, with whom he could joke or sound out on the major problems of the time.

For Jackie it was a time for water skiing or just stretching out in the sun and keeping an eye on the press boat which always came too close for her pleasure and about which she always commented. Sometimes the President slipped over the side for a swim. He wore his back brace and was never photographed until he was submerged to neck level. Once when he swam off the coast of Florida in waters in which sharks had been spotted there was some mild criticism in the press about the President offering himself up so innocently. Kennedy was irritated. "I've been swimming like that ever since I can remember. If a shark hasn't gotten me by this time, I don't think there is much chance of it now." He went on swimming.

The mood of these cruises could always be detected by the laughter which came over the water. There were family jibes about the week's events and the week's people. Kennedy would offer a wry observation about Andrei Gromyko or Senator William Fulbright and seek a response. He was badgered by the children for his fictional accounts of animals and people. He dreamed up one about a white whale that ate socks and was gratified when guest Franklin D. Roosevelt, Jr., took off his shoes, pulled off his socks and threw them overboard to show how the monster demanded feeding. On one hot day the President took Caroline's chocolate ice cream cone and smeared it on her back as she squealed in delight.

When Kennedy first took office he liked to bring his friends in at night after work and take them over to the South Lawn, pointing out the putting green. "Ike could put his golf shoes on at his desk and walk out to practice," he said enviously. In fact, Kennedy had a private yen for the links which he indulged sometimes on the sly.

Since he made such an issue of the putting green he didn't often use it. But he never had it plowed up. When he found he needed more exercise and decided to try golf again in earnest, he had Stoughton come to the Hyannis Golf Club and take slow motion movies of his swing. Stoughton would crouch at a distance and set the camera rolling as Kennedy took his stance. He would keep the film turning until Kennedy had hit the ball and had seen where it went. Then the President would give a hand signal to indicate a good shot, a slice, or a hook. When he saw the film, Kennedy could then match the swing with the results. He drove and putted and pitched and at one time considered gathering up the movie film and calling in a pro to take a look to see just how well he was doing and how he could do better.

The Kennedy golf games were erratic. He would play a couple of holes, cut across the course and come back in for three or four more. Those who played with him never recalled him finishing a full eighteen holes. Golf was fun, but not that serious to Kennedy. He bet a few cents on each hole, was a constant needler and kidder. Maybe the Kennedy fun hit its peak when Press Secretary Pierre Salinger, went along and distinguished himself by driving the ball up and behind the party so that it hit the club house. Kennedy was so tickled by this gaff that he brought it up for weeks, declaring it was the first time in history that such an athletic feat had been achieved on the Hyannis fairways.

In today's atmosphere of heightened security, when no reporters or photographers are allowed to watch the President play golf, it is hard to imagine those rather casual days of Kennedy play. He would start out with friends, maybe a reporter or two in the party, and plug along with the regular flow of golfers, waiting his turn, being doubly cautious about upsetting other players with his Secret Service contingent or the phalanx of cameramen. Once when his brother-in-law Peter Lawford came out on the course at Palm Beach in bare feet, Kennedy was upset. While such casualness might be approved in California, it had no place in the presidential party. Kennedy made that plain.

Kennedy kept up his reading. Friends were sent to gather books when he heard about them or came across them in his persistent study of the newspapers. It is doubtful that he read many volumes from cover to cover during his days in the White House. But he scanned them enough to catch the flavor, to know when to slow down for the meat. Barbara Tuchman's *The Guns of August* intrigued him the most. I remember Kennedy saying one evening that the book more than anything he had read told him what his job in the White House really was—to avoid a sequence of international misunderstandings that would lead to another Apocalypse. Kennedy savored the printed page for its style and language as well as for its content. He liked to talk to authors, to hear good lines and good ideas.

His love of fresh air led him frequently into the Rose Garden. Sometimes when he had a few minutes between appointments and the weather permitted he would idle a bit in the sun, looking at the array of flowers in bloom. One time one of the secretaries was startled as she came out on the arcade between the mansion and the West Wing and saw the President practicing throwing a baseball with aide Dave Powers. He was working up his arm for his pitch-out on baseball's opening day, an athletic ritual of Presidents for decades. Kennedy was determined not to flub his throw. Besides, he liked the brief interlude with Powers, a man far beyond the role of court jester that some assigned him. Powers was a persistent bright spot in any day. He was a link with plain people, a reservoir of basic wisdom and humor. He, too, helped bring release at opportune moments.

The Kennedy fascination with the movie kingdom and with Hollywood characters was a direct legacy from his father Joe Kennedy, who had made part of his fortune in the business. There had always been movies in the Kennedy household when the President was growing up. There were movies in the White House, at Palm Beach and Hyannis, at Camp David, and wherever else the President went. He loved them. They lifted him beyond reality more than anything else. He would sit silently, involving himself with the plot, roaring with laughter at even the corniest jests, sounding his sympathetic critiques for even some of the worst movies. He knew so many of the people who acted in movies that he had no real objectivity.

The movies became an integral part of the Kennedys' private evening entertainment. Many evenings they would have dinner and then gather in front of the screen for the latest Hollywood offering. Once in Palm Beach Stoughton found he had 35mm film and a 16mm projector and the movie plans had to be dropped, much to Jackie's displeasure because she had a house full of guests that evening. They rushed over some 35mm arc light projectors the next day only to have a torrential rain render them useless, since they had to be used outdoors and anyone who turned them on would have risked electrocution. While Jackie did not understand the technical problem, the President did.

The children were allowed to be part of these evenings until their 8 P.M. bedtime. The President even had a popcorn machine installed in the Palm Beach house to create a realistic atmosphere. While he enjoyed any and all movies, he favored adventure films. He naturally developed a special liking for Cliff Robertson who played Kennedy in "Pt 109," and he listened with great interest to Hollywood stories from visitors like Danny Kaye, Judy Garland, and Carol Burnett.

During informal moments before family dinners, Kennedy would often put on a stack of Sinatra records and listen as he sipped a daiquiri. Kennedy liked background music. He supervised the installation of stereo speakers behind the book covers of the Harvard classics in the Oval Living Room upstairs. He had a large speaker installed under his White House bed.

Kennedy painted a bit, he shot skeet at Camp David, sailed a model boat given to Caroline by Italy's President Segni, skippered his sailboat the *Victura* and the Coast Guard sailing sloop *Manitou* on a visit to Maine, watched Jackie ride in Virginia, and walked on the beaches for endless hours. His joys were for the most part very basic—movies and good company, books, beaches and wind and water. They were pursued in the fashion of the very wealthy, the only people who can still claim for themselves stretches of unmarred sand, large, elegant boats, and miles of open country. Kennedy made no excuses for this rich man's environment. He reveled in it with quiet dignity and an appreciation of how lucky he was.

During the America's Cup race off Newport in 1962 Kennedy spotted his Press Secretary Pierre Salinger all bundled up against the brisk weather. He was amused by Salinger's preparations for

his day on the sea and he summoned Stoughton to take a picture. Kennedy removed his own jacket, unbuttoned his collar and loosened his tie and said, "Here, Captain, now shoot this."

On the beach at Hyannisport, the President, Teddy, and Caroline Kennedy watch family friend K. LeMoyne Billings launch the model sailboat given to Caroline by Italy's President Antonio Segni. The maiden cruise was so successful that the Secret Service had to be summoned to go out in one of their power boats to get the model back.

The sun and sea restored John Kennedy's energy and his intellectual equilibrium. Nothing he did pleased him as much as cruising off the Cape. Here, in the summer of 1963, he reads a newspaper while smoking one of his after lunch cigars; he then applies full presidential vigor in an attack on a chocolate ice cream cone. Finally, he squints against a brilliant summer sun reflecting off the water.

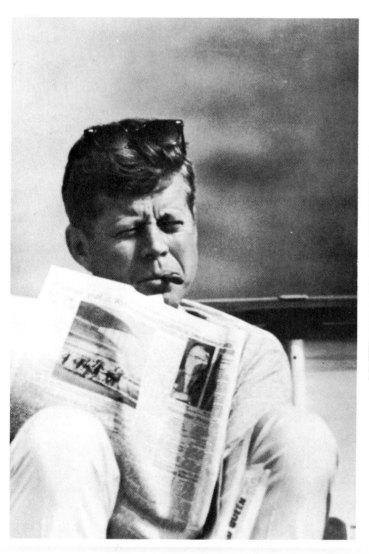

A scene from the famous golf game in which Salinger hit a ball that went behind him and glanced off the club house. This is not that particular bit of action that amused the President so much, but the Salinger form is about the same.

In Palm Beach at Easter 1963 Kennedy amuses John-John in the swimming pool with a hand puppet. Swimming was the President's chief form of exercise and relaxation. In the pool Kennedy could play with the children with far less danger to his injured back.

In Lassen National Park Kennedy went out to feed bread to the deer which came up for handouts from tourists. The next morning when there was no toast with his breakfast he wanted to know why. He was told he had fed the entire supply to the deer.

Caroline's pony Leprechaun nibbles at the presidential ear as family friend Toni Bradlee tries to divert it. Kennedy called out to Stoughton, "Keep shooting, Captain, you are about to see a President being eaten by a horse."

Perfect weather and an American victory helped make the America's Cup races of 1962 a special joy for Kennedy. Above, he and Jackie look out over the flotilla of spectator boats, almost as fascinating as the race itself.

At the Cape, Kennedy loved to board his old boat Victura *when time permitted. Left and right, Kennedy helps adjust the mainsail. His friend Charles Spaulding sits in the stern. Below, the boat scrapes ground as the intrepid skipper and crew misjudge the water and wind. The captain was disgruntled for a few minutes with his and his crew's performance.*

An official meeting with Italy's Prime Minister Fanfani was broken up to take this stroll on the South Lawn where the children were playing. In the foreground, John-John holds a toy dog. Jackie is beside Fanfani who loved the rowdy scene.

Kennedy gives a wave of congratulations to the Weatherly *which has just passed the finish line beating Australia's* Gretel *in the first of the three races.*

Above, now and then in the ceremonial routine there is some fun. Kennedy takes a stance with one of the golf clubs given to Irish Prime Minister Sean Lemass when he visited the United States in October 1963. Lemass is in front of U.S. flag. Protocol Chief Angier Biddle Duke is at right.

THE CHILDREN

"Take my picture, Taptain Toughton." . . . John-John

It was like a transplanted New England village. It seemed designed for children. The father's office was only a short walk away. There were pictures of ships on the walls and scrimshawed whale's teeth decorating his desk. There were innumerable other objects of interest and an extraordinary number of small passageways and anterooms for exploring. Outside their father's door, on the secretary's desk, was a jar filled with rock candy for the small vistors, who almost always traipsed over once or twice a day, sometimes totally unannounced. Only when the most serious business was in progress were they kept out.

So it was that John and Jacqueline Kennedy tried to construct some kind of family life in those acres under glass that form the center of a city devoted to scrutinizing the White House. Looking back, their creation was rather remarkable. Beyond the mansion, where the family lived, and the office where the President worked, were the wooded lawns which got their greatest use by youthful enthusiasts since Teddy Roosevelt led his brood through the thickets and over the gentle swells. Sometimes the pony Macaroni grazed on the lush blue grass, and sometimes he was hitched up for a short trot. There was a tree house and a trampoline, a slide and swings, and countless hideaways in the rhododendrons and under the magnolias. All was the rightful preserve of Caroline and John F. Kennedy, Jr. For Caroline there was even a school on the premises. Her friends came by car pools, and they guzzled milk at recess, and they took short field trips over the lawns. Those ten children in kindergarten and then first grade were hardly aware of the special world they were inhabiting. They have been told by now, of course, and undoubtedly their minds have grasped the significance. But then it was—well, just school.

Sometimes when they were assembled in the walkway between the working wing and the mansion, the President would come through on his way to his office. "Oh, look," they would shout, "here's Caroline's daddy." So much for Presidents. A delighted Kennedy would get bogged down in their midst before he went on to the lofty affairs of state.

While the White House grounds were central to this family, there were other dimensions provided by the jet plane and the fleet of helicopters. The Kennedys used the Virginia countryside for weekends of riding and walking, and for just staying beyond the official grasp. The old family routine of summer at Cape Cod never faltered and there were excursions to Jackie's home, Hammersmith Farm. And there was Palm Beach in the winter. At each place, while climate and activities differed, there was the informality, openness, with the children included in almost everything except the most ceremonial of activities, and even then sometimes they invaded those.

Clifton remembers with relish earnest conversations of instruction which the President had with his son when he grew to a size to venture to the West Wing by himself. The conversations generally concerned candy. John, of course, found Evelyn Lincoln's candy dish the best attraction of the whole presidential business. Only on occasion was it exceeded by the Marine helicopters which churned down onto the South Lawn. The President was concerned about any excessive sweets. When he spotted abuses of the candy privilege he would pause in his chores and reason with the two year old about the need to limit his consumption. He got, according to Stoughton, who watched it all quietly, the usual response to such parental admonitions.

Indeed, Kennedy even had another reason to be proper about such things. He knew other people were constantly watching. He understood the power of example in the Presidency. Thus, he felt compelled to deliver these small lectures on good health and good habits with unusual seriousness. John and Caroline seemed to understand the special predicament of their father and accepted his instructions with a loving tolerance.

Clifton calculated the presence of the children in almost all things. What ceremonies and special events on the lawn or in the White House would interest them, he would ask himself far enough in advance so their attendance could be planned. When they showed up at staff meetings, some Cabinet officers were not certain at first how to take the intrusions. But those like Robert McNamara were delighted. No matter how serious the subject, when Caroline appeared, the Secretary of Defense would halt and give her a grin and a "Hello Caroline." Sometimes she would stand with her arm resting on her father's rocking chair while

John-John shows off his beach robe at Hyannisport, and asks to have his picture taken.

the work went on. Sometimes she would only pause, then slip out.

"When John discovered the trap door on the front of the President's desk he used it as his cave," recalls Clifton. "He would hide there and peek out. There were times when he was playing under the desk when staff members would come in to meet with the President and the meetings would go on despite the play. Now and then you would hear a squeal or a thump from under the desk. If the people there were like Kenny O'Donnell the kids could stay under the desk. Sometimes, if the visitors were not so much a part of the family, the President would call for Dave Powers to come in and take John back to the mansion. Dave was a pal, a companion to those kids. I'd run into him being a soldier or a Marine and marching off with John, sword over his shoulder."

As time went on, Stoughton became a fixture of the inner White House circle. He hovered outside the office door to catch family and business pictures. He arranged with Mrs. Lincoln to have a special buzzer hooked to his desk in the basement so that, when pictures were needed by the President or picture opportunities occurred, he could be summoned. His special joys were the times the kids showed up. "Go on in," Mrs. Lincoln would say, "the children are in there." That meant that informality and perhaps even some confusion was in order and a photographer as quiet and discreet as Stoughton would hardly be seen.

"Take my picture Taptain Toughton," was John's special challenge. Stoughton did it hundreds of times.

"I never made a bad picture of the children. You couldn't. All you had to do was aim the camera and shoot. You always got something. I became such a part of the scene that many times I didn't even need a telephoto lens. I was close enough just to take pictures normally. And they expected it."

To the children the camera was part of a game. Caroline in her fifth and sixth years thought it a perfect delight to make a face every time she saw Stoughton. He has a splendid file of Caroline's funny faces. But Cecil eventually got his way with a little basic psychology. "I've made a picture for you," Stoughton would tell Caroline, after squeezing off a frame or two of her latest face. "Now, let's make one for your Mommy."

After the presence of Stoughton became accepted by the staff, they tipped him off to new developments. One day he came to Evelyn Lincoln's office and noted some special excitement. "Something new today," said Mrs. Lincoln. "John's lost a tooth." Stoughton looked down at the floor where the boy was playing with a model helicopter and a picture of a helicopter. "Where is your tooth," asked Stoughton. There followed a

magnificent grin, the immense void spectacularly displayed for the cameraman's quick finger.

It was of constant fascination to Clifton to watch the President with his children. There was no baby talk. The conversations, while fanciful and concerned with the fundamentals of a child's life, were always adult in tone and outlook. Kennedy suffered no more than the normal parental frustrations, a testimony to the quality of life which Jackie Kennedy somehow maintained even within the White House. Clifton recalls the futile entreaties one time of the President to get his son to go back to the mansion. Kennedy decided to lead the way. Still no deal. John finally sat down and began to cry terribly, from outrage at being so put upon. The President, because of his bad back could not lift his children. He could only use stern language, and he did. While the results were not textbook perfect, the Kennedy Presidency went on, the Republic survived. So did John-John. He even went home.

No opportunity for some bit of education from the special circumstances of the Presidency was allowed to pass if the moment was right. Flying back on *Air Force One* from Cape Cod, the President took Caroline on his lap one day. "Now Caroline, let's see if you can name the New England States," he asked. Carefully and patiently they went over the states. Not once, but several times, until Caroline could tick them off by herself. "What state are you from?" the Preisdent persisted. And then, "What was the first state in the Union? We are now flying over New York State. Where is that?"

Naturally, a man who loved words and language as much as Kennedy hoped to pass on this special passion to his children. They were read to. They were told stories. Kennedy himself was a prime source of stories from the world around the Kennedy family.

"All right daddy," Caroline said once. "Tell me a story. What about a story about bears?" Like other artists, Kennedy tended to focus on the subject matter he knew best. Bears were not his strength. "What about a story about the governors?" he asked. Then he compromised. "Five bears were the governors of five states." It is one of the tragedies of history that this account of the gubernatorial achievements and struggles of the five bears was drowned out by the jet engines and staff work and no account was fully recorded. Certainly, it must be filled with sage political advice as well as basic human wisdom. When the telling of the story was finished, the President, a man who knew the value of audience approval, sought some sign of how well he had done. "How did you like that?" he asked. "Well," said Caroline about the story, "there were five bears instead of three."

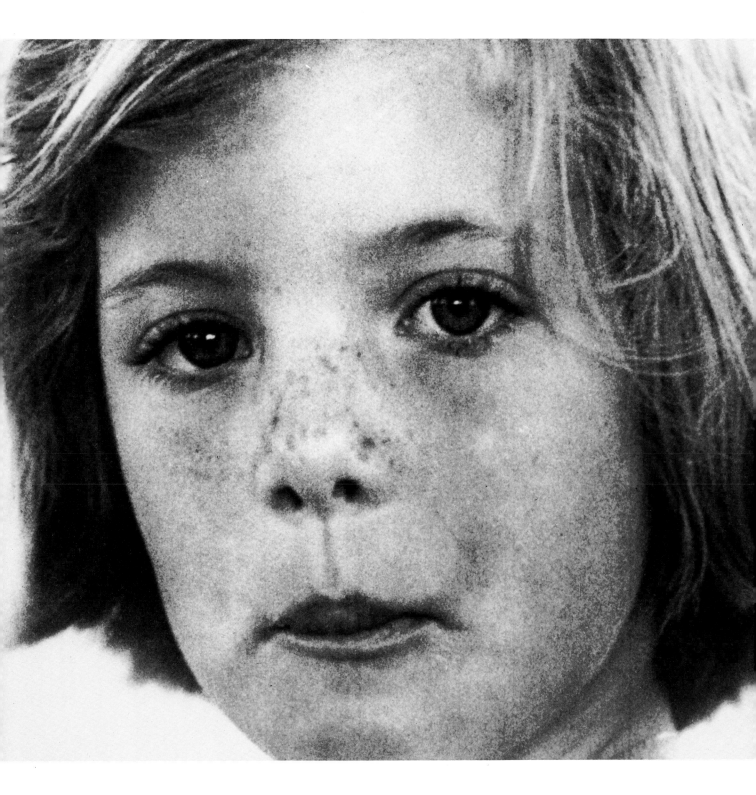

This picture came out of a 16 mm movie. It is a favorite of Jackie's. The footage was made on the Honey Fitz *off the Cape in July of 1963. When Jackie saw the film the following week she asked for an 8 x 10 print from one of the frames of this close-up.*

OVERLEAF *Sandy Eiler, the family's summer athletic counselor, squares off with a tickled John-John on the Cape beach during swimming instruction. White House Aide Dave Powers falls into John-John's close order drill as they emerge from the President's office.*

Above, in the summer of 1962 John-John got help in his outings around the White House grounds. On one, Nurse Maude Shaw stepped aside so that Stoughton could get this picture of a cleaned and combed young man. Right, this picture was taken a year later just before John-John's third birthday. Here, he plays soldier, and, besides learning to march, John-John learned how to salute. This was the weekend before Dallas.

Christmas play in 1962 in Palm Beach. Caroline was Mary, holding the Baby Jesus. Her cousin Christina Radziwill was an angel. And the son of Jackie's personal attendant, Providencia Parades, played Joseph. The play was conceived and produced by Jackie for the special pleasure of Joseph Kennedy.

John-John shows his first-tooth-out smile. He was playing on the floor of Evelyn Lincoln's office with a toy helicopter and a picture of the presidential chopper when Stoughton asked to see the new smile.

Stoughton who was standing outside the President's office on an afternoon in 1963, heard giggling coming from what was supposed to be an empty room. He looked in, spied Caroline and a friend peering out of their "cave" and got this shot.

Another afternoon of play on the south grounds of the White House. Left, Caroline bounces on the trampoline while one of her friends lies bravely underneath. Above, Caroline makes a face at Stoughton. She is riding on a golf cart at Camp David with Secret Service man Bob Foster.

A delegation of candy grabbers, led by Caroline, above and right, come by to ask the President for permission to raid Evelyn Lincoln's candy jar. Nothing less than presidential authority could limit the take to one piece of candy per child.

The only picture in this book not taken by Cecil Stoughton is this one, snapped by John F. Kennedy, Jr., age three. Stoughton shot a picture of John-John playing with the rabbit, then said, "I like rabbits too. How about taking my picture with the rabbit." John-John jumped at the chance and handled Stoughton's wide-angle Hasselblad like a professional.

This twelve picture sequence is perhaps Stoughton's favorite picture story from his Kennedy days. It was recorded in about three minutes one morning in October 1962. As was his habit, Stoughton had stationed himself near the door of Evelyn Lincoln's office. Caroline and John-John came by on one of their excursions that took them first to the favorite candy jar, then in to see their father. Stoughton hefted his cameras into place as he saw the children get a piece of candy, then move on into the Oval Office. "The next thing I knew I heard the President clapping and singing out, 'Hey, here's John-John,'" recalls Stoughton. He moved to the door. They had already started to dance around in a circle on the President's green carpet with the seal in it. "This looks like a fun thing I should be making a picture of," Stoughton said. Kennedy signaled for him to come into the office. Stoughton circled to the left, putting the light from the tall windows to his back. With his wide-angle Hasselblad, he shot the first frame of John-John playing peek with him at the door.

The President kept on clapping and singing. The children thought it was great. They laughed and giggled and began to dance and strut.

Stoughton realized that this sequence was something special. He had the film processed within a couple of hours and took the prints to the President. Kennedy began to laugh again as he looked at the pictures. He chose the picture which he liked best (the last one in this layout) and summoned Salinger, "Why can't we give this one to the press for the birthday picture which they are always demanding?" The picture soon was all over the world. Sometime later, Stoughton took a copy of this print and asked Kennedy to autograph it. While Stoughton stood there Kennedy penned the message shown.

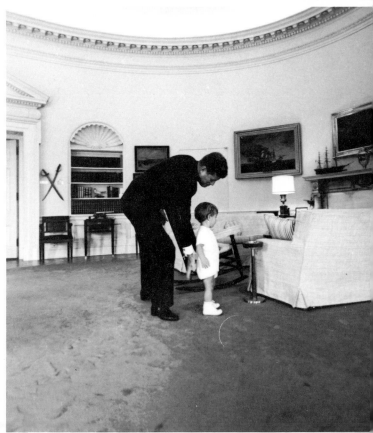

daughters — who captured beautifully
a happy moment at the White House —

Jackie

158

"Everything in the White House must have a reason for being there..." ... Jacqueline Kennedy

There are twenty-two rooms in the big old house which James Hoban designed, which George Washington ordered built, and of which John Adams became the first resident. There are another thirty-four rooms combined in the West Wing (built by Teddy Roosevelt) and the East Wing (built by his cousin Franklin Roosevelt), with the eighteen acres of lawns and gardens. Both the President and his wife thought that the beauty and dignity of the White House were a necessary part of the spectacle of the Presidency, that as many Americans as possible ought to see how the White House looked, how it was being used. Though small in size compared to the vast castles of Europe, its simple elegance was a splendid backdrop.

Jackie wanted it to be even better. She wanted it restored to the manner that Jefferson and Madison (the two tasteful Virginians who did most to set the White House style) had planned, to become a kind of living museum which drew its basic character from the beginning, but which received a special and personal accent from each of its inhabitants. The refurbishing was a success and has been chronicled in detail over the years. But it was more than just new furniture and new wallpaper.

In the summer of 1963 Jackie sent Stoughton a note asking that he make a complete record of the White House rooms. She wanted the rooms as they looked when idle. She wanted pictures of the people in them. She wanted everything from the pantry to the East Room.

It was this assignment that produced the pictures which follow. They show the formal White House and the White House in which the Kennedys lived as a family in their last months of residence. It is a photographic record that has not been seen before. Stoughton took the pictures one weekend when the Kennedys were in Hyannisport. The rooms had become reflections of the Kennedy personality. They were a mixture of the memorabilia of the family and the French furniture that Jackie loved so much. There were paintings of American Indians on the wall and there were stuffed teddy bears on the floor. There was Winnie the Pooh and a Renoir borrowed from the Corcoran Gallery. It was functional but graceful, historical but livable.

On one morning John Kennedy had some of his key Cabinet officers to breakfast in the family dining room (the small dining room on the first floor which, along with other official rooms, was restored as Jefferson and Madison had designed it). A dozen antique dining room chairs had been placed around the table. In the midst of his concerns of state, Kennedy leaned back on his chair. According to witnesses, the chair exploded beneath him. One brace snapped and the whole chair disintegrated. His aide, Larry O'Brien, helped him up and they pushed another of the valuable antiques into service. Kennedy just a bit shaken, resumed his discussion. Once again he pushed back on two hind legs, and another antique chair collapsed. By this time his poise was a bit frayed. There were some eloquent swear words and he suggested that henceforth they get chairs which would support men rather than those whose chief value was their age and frailty.

For the most part, however, Jackie's antiques were not only historic but, restored and soundly glued, they functioned perfectly. She was justly proud of the White House she had re-created.

From the niches where the children's toys were piled to the grand state dinners for 150 glittering personalities, Stoughton roamed with his cameras in hand. His problems were those of lighting, of huge groups of people, of quick movements of subjects who were most often unsympathetic to his requirements. In those years there was no formal recognition of the need for a photographic record. In later years there was, and special lighting, a special photographic laboratory, and various assistants were provided. But when Stoughton came on the scene, he was a lonely intruder, in a strange world.

One of the curious facts of life with John Kennedy was that he was rather uncomfortable in front of a camera even though he recognized the need for and the use of it. It is one of those ironies of history that many still believe Kennedy overexploited the visual aspects of his Presidency, when in reality Presidents Nixon and Johnson were much more attentive to the powers of the camera.

Stoughton was never personally close to either of the Kennedys. He had not been an old friend. He was not brought into the most intimate circle during his White House days. He was on duty as a photographer, doing what he had done all his life. That he became a devoted follower and participant is true. That the work he did required that he be closer to the First Couple than most others is true as well. But he was a silent worker, refusing to intrude personally, reaching out with his lens to grasp the moment. Thus, his photographic record is all the more remarkable. He expanded his limits in subtle ways. He pressed his reserves of energy and time.

When the buzzer on his basement desk sounded he never knew if he would be required to photograph a single politician shaking hands with the President or whether it might be fifty nuns from Shannon. His wide-angle Hasselblad was his right arm. It could cover any subject from two feet to fifty and it could do it in a few seconds.

Stoughton learned the presidential signals. Kennedy never allowed more than a couple of frames to be taken; he didn't want time wasted. He listened for two clicks and then, even when a worried Stoughton would quietly ask for "one more," most often the President had already turned and would be striding off by the time the third shot could be taken. For Stoughton a nod of the presidential head meant leave. A particular glance also meant the picture-taking was over. Among Kennedy's pet hates were the political lineups where he would grip a congressman's hand for the campaign picture that each candidate treasured for the local papers. Stoughton learned to take those pictures so fast that the visitors standing beside the President didn't know it had started, when it was over, and Kennedy was moving on.

Jackie, who had once been a photographer for the Washington *Times Herald*, had a far better appreciation, both for the technical problems of picture-taking and for the use of the pictures. She wanted a record of White House rooms and activities for history. She understood the importance of camera angles. She asked Stoughton, for instance, "Don't make pictures of Jack and me. Make pictures of what we are looking at and what we are doing." Many of Stoughton's pic-

tures are taken over the shoulders of the couple in cognizance of that command. After viewing Stoughton's movies of the Kennedy tour of Europe in the summer of 1963, Jackie told him that he had been placed too far back in some of the motorcades. Henceforth, she decreed, he was to ride behind the presidential car where he could capture the emotion on the faces of the people as the President passed.

Jackie understood motion picture scripts. There were certain activities which she saw and made mental notes about, later to dispatch memos to Stoughton about when and where to shoot. ("The President Saturday A.M. at the farm with Caroline . . . another weekend inside helicopter with children and President.")

Once he was even sent to New York to a fashion show at Chez Ninon. Because Jackie's presence at such things was so disruptive both of the event and herself, she seized on the idea of having Stoughton take pictures of the gowns being modeled, bringing back samples of the fabrics. He was the only man present in September 1962, but, undaunted, he performed beautifully. He arranged himself so that in one picture he not only photographed the front of each dress being modeled, but got a rear view from a full-length mirror strategically placed. Jackie wrote her praise and thanks, adding "Don't leave us for Harper's Bazaar."

There were times when Stoughton began to think he really was in Camelot. We word men who have tried over the years to discourage the use of that term, nevertheless, get a twinge or two of the same emotion when we listen again to the stories of those moments of special joy.

For instance, Stoughton recounts those nights when the big dinners were on. He would don his rented white tie and tails and he would melt into the walls with his cameras. There was much laughter and the Marine Band would strike up a lively tune and the polished chandeliers would glow in the soft light. He worked in a kind of magnificent trance. When it was over he would go down to the kitchen to see his friend René Verdon, the chef. René knew what to do. He took the choice leftovers, a bottle of, say, Haut-Brion 1953 that had not been drunk, and set this all out for himself, Stoughton, and Ferdinand Louvat the pastry chef. There they would dine like prime ministers, and amid the pots and pans they would raise their glasses, filled with the superb vintages, to the President, to whom they were devoted.

OVERLEAF *Jackie drives the small sleigh up the South Lawn in December 1962. Caroline and a friend ride along and her pony Macaroni pulls the sleigh. Jackie chose this picture to put on the John F. Kennedys' personal Christmas card that year.*

Left, Jackie and John-John watch from the door of the diplomatic reception room as the President lifts off the South Lawn in his helicopter.

Above, a collection of John-John's playthings photographed in the nursery.

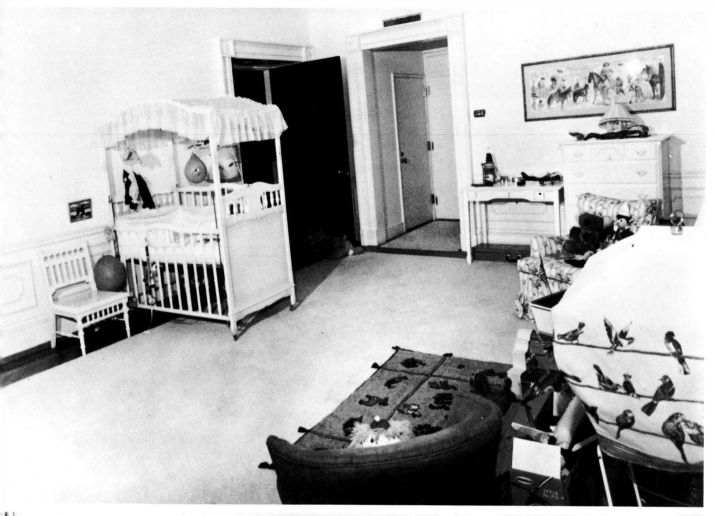

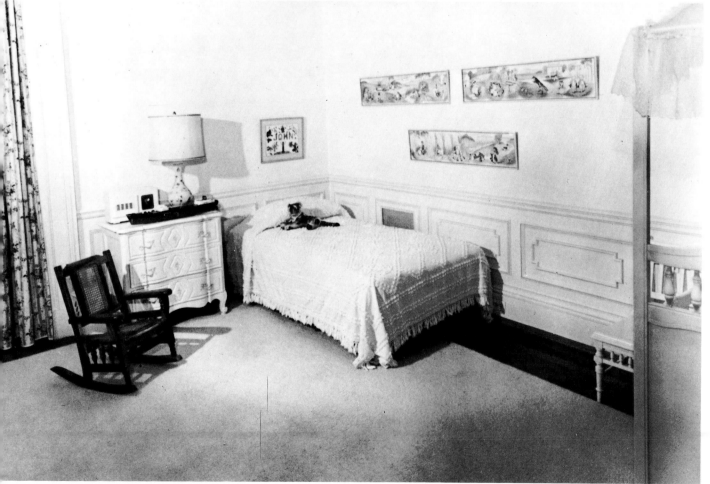

Three views of the children's nursery on the second floor of the mansion. John-John occupied the crib, Caroline the low bed with the stuffed tiger on it. Their dolls and stuffed animals were on display near the fireplace. When these pictures were taken the parakeet was under his cover.

Below, this ninety-seven foot mural painted by Bernard Lamotte on the walls of the swimming pool was a gift to the President from his father. The scene is St. Croix in the Virgin Islands.

Above right, the President's bedroom which includes another of his special rockers and his books collected on the table at the end of the bed.

Right, Jackie's bedroom, decorated with special care by the First Lady. Windows look out over the South Lawn. An adjoining sitting room, overlooks the President's office.

Below, the small dining room on the first floor near the State Dining Room. Known as the family dining room, Kennedy held his business breakfasts and lunches here.

OVERLEAF *Jackie's special pride was the gold Oval Room on the second floor of the mansion. Here it is shown restored. From it one goes out to the Truman balcony and has the view, across the South Lawn, of the Washington Monument and the Jefferson Memorial.*

The Blue Room on the first floor of the mansion, as restored by Jackie.

THE PARENTS

"Hurry up Caroline, I want to use the phone."

... The President

The encompassing problem for the President and his wife as parents was to somehow carve out a normal family environment, or something approaching it, from a thoroughly abnormal situation. Around every corner of that fishbowl was another problem, a threat to family serenity and privacy, two very necessary ingredients of stability.

Jackie was determined to hold photographers as far away as possible in the early years, even though there was more pressure from more photographers than ever before to come into the inner family circle and record it for the millions of Kennedy fans. A lucky shot of the children playing brought near mayhem in the press. Other less fortunate cameramen raised protests and cried for equal footage. CBS's Bruce Hoertell, for instance, had come to work innocently enough on the Ellipse one snowy morning in November 1962 and he caught sight of Jackie driving the tiny sleigh across the White House lawn. He stuck his camera through the fence and recorded some of the most charming White House footage ever seen. The outcry from the White House press corps was tremendous. The only response which Pierre Salinger could concoct was to pass out some copies of still pictures of the same scene which Stoughton had snapped. Jackie's rules about the children were firm. They bent occasionally to be sure, and now and then they were even breached, but by calculation. For the most part they held.

The White House life for Caroline and John-John was fiercely normalized. But it seemed to work. The children were cheery, bright, and unself-conscious as they moved through their special world. While there was a nurse and many White House servants, Jackie did more mothering than most people realized. She strolled down the South Lawn on the sunny days with John-John still in the carriage. She romped with Caroline on the grass and sent for the pony Macaroni so Caroline could learn to ride as she, Jackie, had done. Jackie changed childrens' clothes and washed dirty hands and faces. She snapped pajamas and read bedtime stories. She hovered over these two most of the days of White House life, trying to assure that the White House neither smothered them nor inflated them.

When it came time for Caroline to go to preschool, Jackie experimented and sent her beyond the White House fence. She found that too disruptive for everybody involved. Secrecy was hopeless. So was privacy. The solution became the White House's own school, with a teacher and a dozen pupils, car pools, and everything else that could be found on the outside.

Had the Kennedys wanted to unloose the flood of affection which the nation had for the children, the results would have been staggering. As it was, gifts poured in constantly from plain citizens as well as heads of state. People reached for pleasure and privilege through the children. All, except gifts from old friends, were turned aside. Birthday cakes baked in Grand Rapids and rocking horses from California were tagged and shipped off to the orphanages and children's hospitals in Washington. In fact, the number of toys allowed the Kennedy children in general, including from family, was rather limited.

As in other phases of White House life, the emphasis in the nursery was on the quality of human relationships. While the children were watched closely and supervised critically, they were not waited on nor coddled beyond infancy. They were lavished with affection and love, but in adult language and reason.

The indulgences were the traditional ones—birthdays, Christmases, Easters. These had always been special family times for the Kennedys, when games and fun were more important than presents. Jackie planned meticulously for these events. On one of Caroline's birthdays there were tricycle races along the basement corridor of the White House. There were movie cartoons in the theater, and then finally, on the family floor, there was the traditional cake and ice cream. For the twenty-five or thirty children who attended, it all seemed normal enough. They brought their presents and handed them to an eager little girl, who dropped on her knees and ripped the paper off expertly, held each gift for all to see and exclaim ever properly.

At Christmas there was a family pageant at Palm Beach which included cousins and anybody else. There were songs and costumes and the story was, naturally, about Mary and Joseph and the Baby Jesus. The drama ended with the participants harnessed up as reindeer prancing off with thoughts of presents undoubtedly dancing in their heads. The author of the play— Jackie Kennedy. It was a mixture of religion and legend, of family and friends.

At Easter time there were eggs to be decorated. When Halloween came, a couple of goblin costumes appeared. On this occasion pictures were allowed as Caroline and John-John stopped by the Oval Office to spook their father before they went off on a secret trick and treat route in Georgetown.

The children's play and parties were mixed with the adult world. Caroline and John-John were encouraged to go on discreet visits to their father's office as much as twice a day. They watched from the Truman Balcony as the dignitaries arrived on the South Lawn and the troops marched and the guns boomed out their salutes. They could stay up with the family friends and watch part of the movies, but when bedtime came around they were firmly marched off. On the great evenings of the state dinners, when the most honored guests and the highest government officials gathered in the Oval Living Room for cocktails before descending the stairs with the President for the reception line, the children were permitted to come to meet the visitors and say good night.

Perhaps he did not perform the services in typical fashion, but the President of the United States on more than one occasion was a babysitter. If he changed diapers, that has not been recorded. If he gave either child a bottle that, too, has escaped the historians. But it is not inconceivable. More than once when Jackie was gone, the President had a lunchtime rendezvous with his children. It was then his job to see that they were behaving properly, to make certain they were well, to provide them with whatever parental guidance seemed appropriate.

In the Spring of 1962 when Jackie was on her Asian tour for almost a month, the President took his babysitting most seriously. Clifton recalls that he considered it just as vital as any other business that he get back to the mansion at noon to check on the children. And every night Kennedy would write his wife a letter bringing her up to date not only on the affairs of state of that day, but also on the affairs of Caroline and John-John.

John Kennedy's lame back prevented him from roughhousing his children on impulse. But sometimes he would lie on the floor of the family living room and let John-John climb over him. When he was

seated on the boat or even at his desk he would often find Caroline in his lap. That kind of affection was never overdone in public. But the love was there. The children knew it and felt it.

These family pictures were not posed. They just happened. Many of the best photographs were taken at moments when nobody could plan for them or predict them. Hair was blowing, clothes were rumpled. Many a time Stoughton stopped taking pictures, concerned about too much informality. He saw Jackie sweep up her son sticky with ice cream or wet from swimming and squeeze him. And sometimes it went the other way. She would come out of the water dripping and clutch a dry Caroline in a hug.

Even in the uncertain routine of the Presidency there were rituals that were established by the children which the adults were expected to live up to. One was the Friday night visit to the candystore in Hyannis. Jackie and the children generally went to the Cape in July and stayed the rest of the summer. The President commuted on Mondays and Fridays. By Friday night it was his turn to lead the troop to the confectioner. Sometimes he was not even allowed to go into his home to change clothes for this essential business. As soon as his motorcade halted in front of the Kennedy house he was commandeered for the candy trip with, "It's your turn to pay." Kennedy rarely had any pocket money for these events and had to borrow from Clifton or a Secret Service agent. And he kept a stern eye on the candy consumption. One five-cent treat was allowed for each member of the gang.

As the children grew older and the Kennedys saw that they could manage the atmosphere of the White House, they relaxed the rules some. Once the President invited in a friendly photographer to shoot pictures of the kids playing in his office. And Caroline found increasing reasons to journey beyond the iron gates with her friends.

There was a time when Kennedy became concerned about John-John's fascination with guns, swords, military uniforms, and anything of a martial nature. He indulged the fancy even as he worried, buying more toy guns and letting him watch the military ceremonies. "I guess we all go through that," said Kennedy wisely. "He just sees more of the real thing."

OVERLEAF *In mid-August of 1963 after the tragic premature birth and death of Patrick B. Kennedy, Jackie came home from the hospital to a special family welcome. At the President's direction both children and all their nine dogs, only some of which are shown here, gathered on the patio of their Squaw Island home to greet her.*

174

Left, Jackie lights the candle on Caroline's cake on her fifth birthday. This part of the party was held in the private dining room on the second floor of the mansion.

Above, John-John gets a short helicopter ride with his father. The President was going from the Kennedy Hyannisport compound to Otis Air Force Base to return to Washington. John-John got to go as far as Otis and back.

Left, a rare family portrait in the fall of 1962. Stoughton was shooting pictures of Jackie and the children. The President happened by, and was induced into the scene by his wife.

Above, Christmas Eve at the Palm Beach White House in 1962. Kennedy hangs up the stockings, then he and Jackie play with the children before they are sent off to bed.

Left, another storytelling session on board the Honey Fitz. *This time Caroline looks a little more skeptical about her father's tale. Below, a typical youthful escort as the President heads for his helicopter to leave Hyannisport for Washington during the summer of 1963. John-John's worried look suggests he might not get to go along.*

Left, a moment at Wexford in Virginia on the weekend before Dallas. John-John has taken a break from soldierly duties to talk things over with his father. Below, in Palm Beach on the eve of Easter, 1963, the children and a friend, Sally Fay, decorate eggs for the next day's celebration.

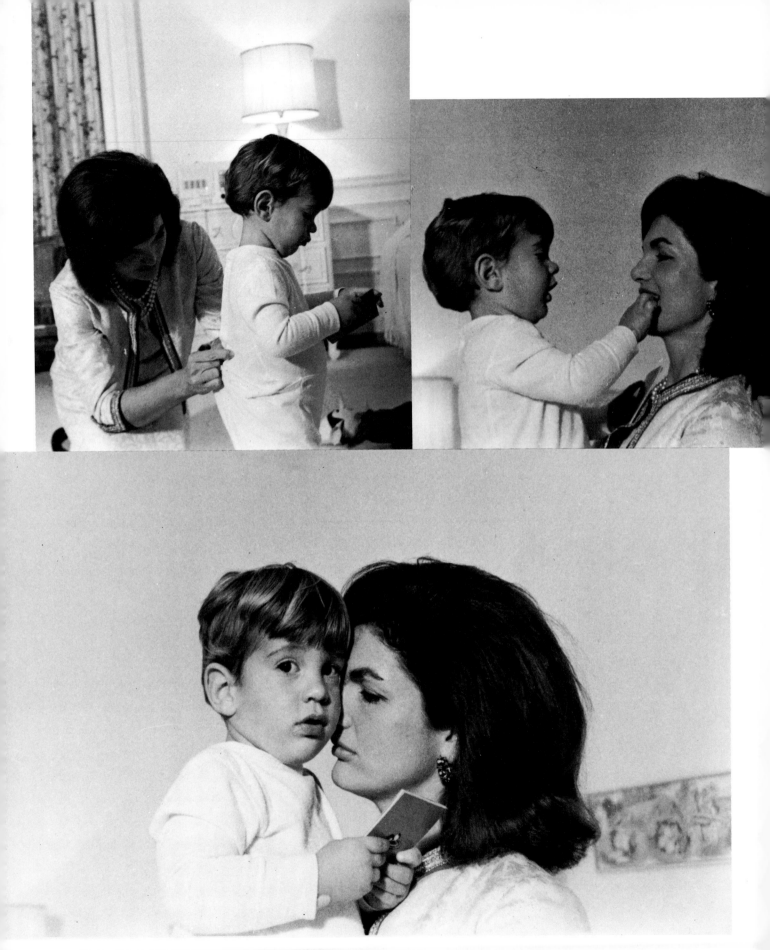

Evening in the nursery. John-John nearly two, gets his pajamas snapped and some special attention from his mother on his way to bed, which also includes a pause for some stories with Caroline.

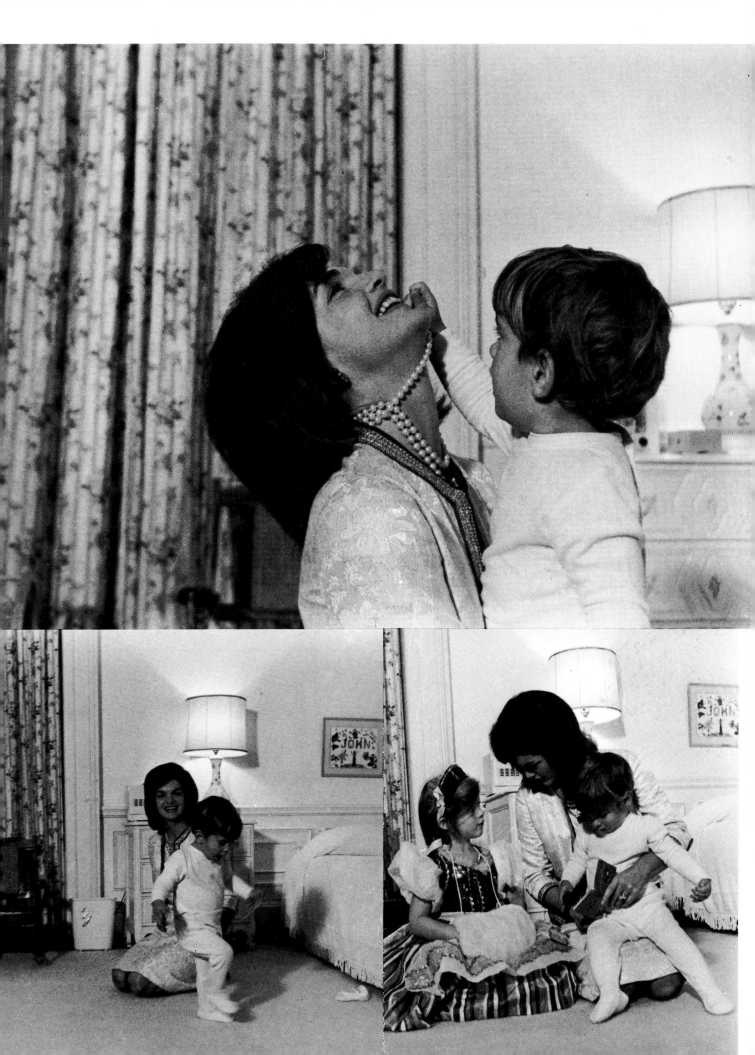

Two Easter portraits. Left, in 1962 the family did not pause for Stoughton as they emerged from Easter services in the parental chapel. Jackie asked Stoughton for a better picture in 1963. He suggested that she have the family pause a moment at the door. She did, and the picture is below.

Right, on a pleasant day in the spring of 1963 the President and John-John play with a ceramic horse on the porch outside his office.

Father and son out for a stroll on the South Lawn in the summer of 1963.

Below, Caroline has an intimate moment with her grandfather, Joseph Kennedy, on the porch of his home. The former Ambassador was almost always on the porch when the President was arriving or leaving.

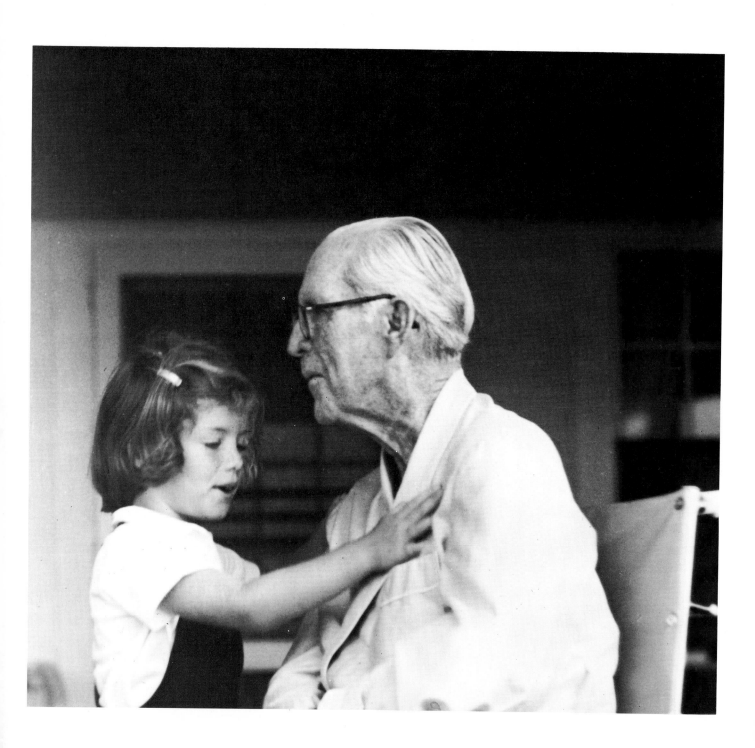

Right, this family picture was taken by Stoughton at Jackie's request. She gave the picture to family friend Morton Downey, whose place they used in the summer of 1962 on the Cape.

An earnest father-daughter discussion. Stoughton captured this moving moment with a long lens, on one of the summer cruises aboard the **Honey Fitz.**

Kennedy was a good storyteller most times. But on some days he asked his children to make up their own stories and tell him. He was an excellent listener.

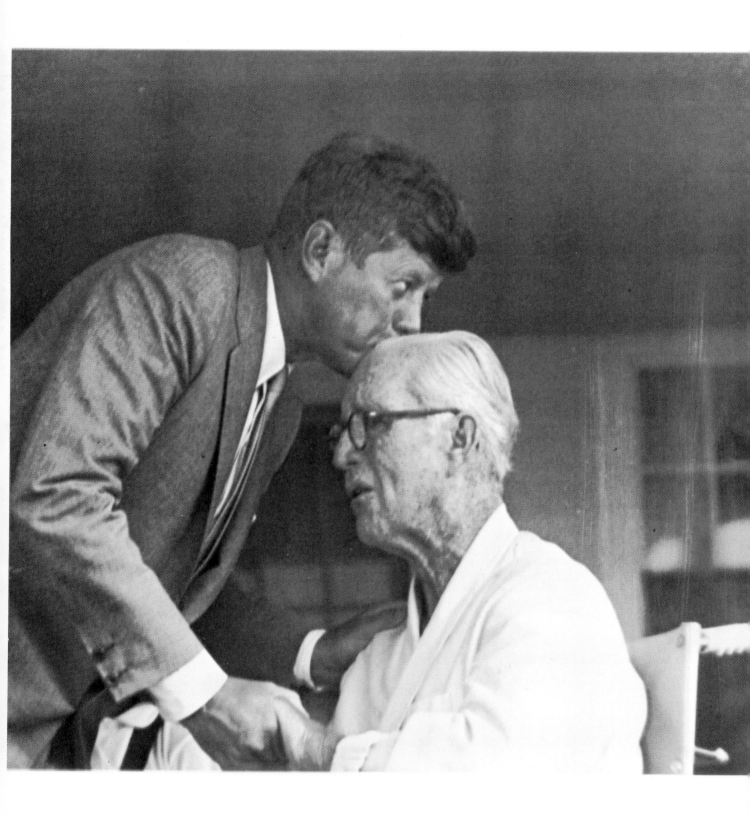

Every time the President left the Cape on Monday morning to return to Washington, he said good-by to his father in this manner. Only in the worst weather, did Joseph Kennedy stay inside. The helicopters used the elder Kennedy's front lawn as a pad during the presidential visits.

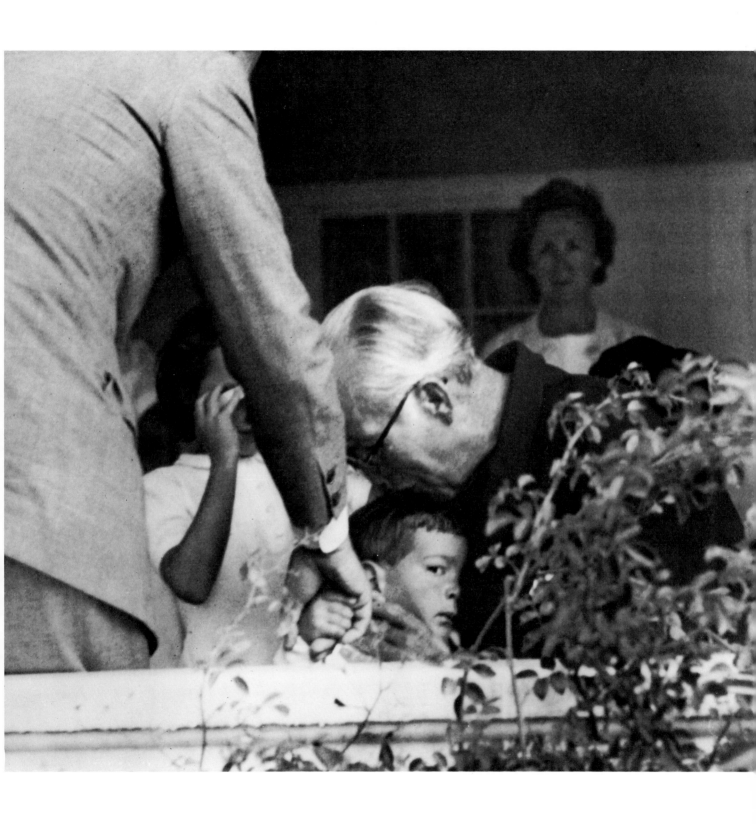

John-John also shared in the farewell rituals. Here he receives a grandfatherly peck and hug, and at the same time retains a tight grip on his father's hand.

In the winter of 1962, Kennedy heard sounds outside the Oval Office and couldn't resist a visit. Stoughton caught this scene as mother, son, and dog came over for a presidential conference.

HE PAUSED ALONG HIS SWIFT JOURNEY

Among the many myths that cling to the Presidency is the one which suggests that the President is the most burdened and abused person in the nation. It is taken as an elemental truth by university students and barbershop philosophers alike that the problems of American Presidents are mostly insoluble and certainly beyond the ken of most individuals. The early Presidents cast the office in bittersweet terms, thereby spawning the belief. "A splendid misery," said Thomas Jefferson. "A crown of thorns," insisted the dour James Buchanan.

For men who deal in power it is the ultimate arena. It is no more frightening to a lusty politician to aspire to the White House than it is for a corporate vice-president in charge of sales to want to become president of his firm. This is not to diminish the Presidency or its burdens. It is, instead, to put it into a human context. Each Presidency is shaped by a man. It is neither greater nor lesser than that man.

John Kennedy sought the scene of action.

Sometimes he seemed almost embarrassed at his own pleasure in being President, and he tried to cover it with humor. It just wasn't quite right to enjoy a job that tradition suggested was filled with pain and anguish so much, so obviously. He came off his plane one day in Newport, Rhode Island, as the Navy Band played "Hail to the Chief." He had a special look of satisfaction on his face as he stood in the bright sun, the flag whipping in a breeze off Narragansett Bay. Perhaps he saw how some of us were smiling at his apparent self-satisfaction. He grinned too, and as the last notes trailed off, he came over to us, leaned close, and muttered, "Don't you love the beat of that piece." He laughed out loud at his own joke and strode off, head up, savoring the salt tang, the surrounding panoply, and his own power.

One time down in the basement of the White House, McGeorge Bundy chortled quietly over Kennedy's self-esteem. It took a special man, said Bundy (no self-doubter himself) to think that he could cope with the world's problems. Indeed, Kennedy took his place with Jefferson and Jackson and the Roosevelts without hesitation. He was a little awed with Lincoln and left him on a pedestal by himself more often than not, but in the others he found kindred spirits. He used their words, stole some of their thoughts, invoked their ghosts in the name of his New Frontier. Maybe he explained it the day he looked out over the South Lawn of the White House and said, "I figure if you set out to be second best, that's the way you will end up."

It was a curious fact that Kennedy was never overly optimistic about the eventual fate of mankind. He wondered if nations like the United States and the Soviet Union could go on building weapons and not at some point feel compelled to use them simply because they were there. Yet he never ceased trying to find some formula for peace, to seize upon those traits of human nobility that sometimes emerged. "Oh, no," he said when asked about his fatalism, "you've got to go on trying." It was, perhaps, his search for excellence coupled with his realization of the human frailties that gave Kennedy the special tolerance which was part of his strength and appeal. There was no person, no institution, no tradition, or episode that did not in some way evoke an effort at understanding.

He proclaimed the New Frontier to be the preserve of youth. In Vienna he told Nikita Khrushchev, who had declared that America was old and worn out and Russia new and rising, to look across the table and he would see just how old America was. But at the same time Kennedy savored an evening with the ancient political hacks of Massachusetts and he liked an hour or two occasionally with Chicago's old-line Mayor Richard Daley. He exalted in youth. He respected age. "What do I call Henry Luce," he once asked me preceding a visit of the aging editor and publisher. "Henry? Harry? He's always been Mr. Luce to me and that is what I'm going to keep on calling him." He did.

While Kennedy was appalled at Khrushchev's seeming indifference to what might happen to civilization if the USSR and U.S. unleashed their nuclear weapons, he was at the time captivated by the man himself. He probed his personality, he studied his words, he looked at his clothes and his hands and his movements.

In the heat of his anger over steel price increases he called the big steel men SOBs and in particular U.S. Steel's Roger Blough, the man he felt had betrayed him because Blough had come to the White House to talk about holding prices in check and at the same time had been silent about his intentions. But when that crisis had passed, Blough became a regular consultant in the Oval Office, a friend of sorts of the President. "There are no permanent enemies in politics," Kennedy mused.

His office was open to as many as he could accommodate in his waking hours. So was his mind and his heart. Bobby Kennedy told the story of the dark days of 1961 when the Berlin Wall went up and the possibility of nuclear war entered John Kennedy's conversation. His special horror was that children would be annihilated in something they had not created, knew nothing about, could not prevent. In those moments he rededicated himself to searching for reason in the nuclear age.

All of this was a part of Kennedy—confidence tempered with doubt, anger followed by tolerance, openness and curiosity and understanding. He touched something in each of us. It was as if he had paused along his swift journey and listened and understood.

OVERLEAF *At noon on December 6, 1963, Jackie, Caroline, and John, Jr., leave the White House for the last time.*

ACKNOWLEDGMENTS

From the beginning we three had struck up a friendship which has endured and has resulted in this book. But, at least one hundred friends have contributed to this book and we only wish that the photographs could reveal all of them and the captions could identify each and every one. There are undoubtedly omissions, but there is no intentional slight either by word or picture, and we hope that every one of our colleagues and friends who will see this book can enjoy it.

Cecil Stoughton must have taken more than eight thousand "frames" of the Kennedy days in the White House. As any photographer will do, when he had taken five, ten, or fifteen fast exposures, he then picked one, two, or three or four and had them printed for the record. Ultimately, he came up with three or four thousand pictures to choose from. For this collection, he skillfully sorted out—based on his own interest as well as his artistic eye—perhaps a thousand.

And then, good fortune came to his elbow. Evan Thomas, our editor at W. W. Norton, brought Emma Landau, Art Director for *American Heritage* magazine to the group. It was she who helped in the selection of two hundred pictures, the best of which are printed here. There were some difficult choices: Many of the great pictures in color had to give way to be shown in black and white. The departments of the Presidency—carefully suggested by Evan—then had to be matched with the pictures. Emma put her mind, and her great imagination—yes, and her dedication—to work, and created the layouts which relate with the ideas—actually, with the people and events, about which this book is written.

Evan and Emma shepherded a sensitive photographer-author through this first "monument" and coordinated the personalities and personal attachments of the three of us.

The reader will note that neither pictures nor text cover the assassination of the President nor the preparations for the funeral, nor any of the awesome events of those trying first days of the transition. But all three of us were with the President and the First Lady on that trip, and during those sorrowful days Stoughton continued to photograph every moment and was on hand when John F. Kennedy's body was brought back to the East Room of the White House in the early morning hours.

From the hospital in Dallas, Ted Clifton commandeered the emergency telephone communication to alert Secretary McNamara and the National Defense Command Post of the tragedy and with the "black bag" found the Vice-President to be sure decisions could be made. He accompanied President Kennedy's body and Mrs. Kennedy on *Air Force One* to Washington and spent the entire night with Sargent Shriver and other staff people on the funeral arrangements, as well as keeping track of the world-wide intelligence for Lyndon Johnson.

Hugh Sidey never stopped filing his copy of the trip and its awful events for both *Life* and *Time*.

So the omission is intentional because we want this book to be an entirely happy memory, and because we know that every person in the world can rely on his or her own memory of those events, and where they were and what they were doing at the moment they heard of the tragedy.

STOUGHTON

Cecil Stoughton began his career as a photographer in 1940 when he voluntarily enlisted in the Army Air Corps from Oskaloosa, Iowa, and asked for a combat photographer's assignment. They put a camera in his hand, sent him to a *Life* magazine training session, and assigned him to the South Pacific Theater of Operations. By 1947 he had decided to make the armed forces and photography his career. He served in Hawaii until 1951. He served with MATS, the Military Air Transport Service, in the Pacific Theater. In 1951 he was assigned to the Joint Chiefs of Staff as a motion-picture photographer and under the supervision of the Office of the Secretary of Defense.

In 1954 he went on the shakedown cruise of the *U.S.S. Nautilus* and claims to be the first Air Force person to move under nuclear power. Master Sergeant Stoughton in 1957 accepted a direct commission in the Army Signal Corps as a First Lieutenant officer-photographer. Shortly thereafter, when Ted

Clifton, then the Deputy Chief of Information of the Army was hunting for a skilled photography man to work with the U.S. Army's burgeoning missile command, Cecil Stoughton became the officer-photographer in Huntsville with Dr. Werner von Braun, photographing significant launches from Cape Canaveral. He was on duty at the Cape when the first successful satellite was launched. In 1961 when Clifton was asked to become President Kennedy's Military Aide, he asked that Cecil Stoughton be assigned to the White House.

For a year after President Kennedy's death, Cecil Stoughton remained at the White House with President Johnson. When Major Stoughton retired from his Army career in April 1967, he became the chief photographer for the National Park Service in the Department of the Interior. And when he retired from the Civil Service in April 1973, he had his first opportunity to create this book.

CLIFTON

Major General Chester V. (Ted) Clifton was selected by President Kennedy as his Military Aide at the outset of his Administration and was continued in that assignment by President Johnson. In August 1965 President Johnson awarded General Clifton the Distinguished Service Medal in a White House retirement ceremony that closed a twenty-nine-year Army career.

Clifton was born in Edmonton, Alberta, Canada, September 24, 1913, of American parents. When he was six years old they moved to Seattle, Washington. After graduating from high school in 1930, he was a cub reporter on the Seattle *Post-Intelligencer* from 1930 to 1932. He was appointed to the United States Military Academy, in 1932. Upon graduation in 1936, he was commissioned a second lieutenant of field artillery. During graduation leave that summer, he served as a general assignment reporter on the staff of the New York *Herald Tribune*. That fall he reported to Fort Sill, Oklahoma.

Following tours of duty there, and in Hawaii, in May 1941, he reported for duty with the 79th Field Artillery at Fort Bragg, North Carolina. In July 1942, he assumed command of the 2nd Battalion, 79th Field Artillery, which became the 698th Field Artillery Battalion (240 mm Howitzers). Moving to Italy in December 1943, Clifton commanded this battalion of the Army's largest artillery weapons, in the North Appenines and the Anzio campaigns. The unit moved to France and Germany and fought in the Ardennes-Alsace, Central Europe, and Rhineland campaigns.

In June 1948, he graduated in the Army Advanced Schooling program from the University of Wisconsin, with an M.A. (Journalism). He joined General Omar N. Bradley's staff and, when Bradley became the first Chairman of the Joint Chiefs of Staff, in August 1949, he was named as an assistant and served with him until August 1953.

Following graduation in 1954, from the National War College, he served a year of command duty in Europe, and then was assigned as Chief, Joint Plans, for the European Command in Paris. Subsequently he was Deputy Chief of Information, Department of the Army. In January 1961, he became Military Aide to President Kennedy.

SIDEY

Hugh Sidey is a fourth-generation journalist. His great-grandfather founded the *Adair County Free Press*, a weekly paper in Greenfield, Iowa, which was subsequently owned and operated by his grandfather and now is run by his father and brother.

While he still was in grade school, Sidey learned the mechanical end of the business—feeding presses, setting type, and sweeping floors. Later, he sold ads, wrote stories, took pictures and made the photoengravings. After a hitch in the Army (he was an enlisted instructor of West Point cadets) he completed his education at Iowa State College, then moved to Washington.

En route, Sidey worked on the Council Bluffs (Iowa) *Nonpareil*, where he covered every type of story, then moved across the Missouri River to the Omaha (Nebraska) *World-Herald*, reporting from city hall for the next four years.

His next move was to a two-year stint with *Life* in New York, then to *Time* magazine in Washington, D.C. He remained in Washington, as White House correspondent and Deputy Chief of the *Time-Life* Washington News Bureau. On January 1, 1969, he became Bureau Chief.

In 1960 Sidey traveled with Presidential Candidate John F. Kennedy on his campaign trail and was one of the reporters in Dallas with the presidential party three years later when President Kennedy was assassinated. During the summer of 1963, Sidey's book *John F. Kennedy, President: A Reporter's Inside Story* was published and quickly made the best-seller list. After the assassination in November 1963, the book was reissued and selected as a Literary Guild alternate selection. It was also serialized in Australia, Great Britain, France, Italy, Japan, Sweden, and Finland.

In April 1966, *Life* started the publication of a by-lined column by Sidey on "The Presidency," in which he reported on the Johnson and Nixon Administrations. The column was transferred to *Time* when *Life* ceased publication. He has accompanied both Presidents on their trips abroad and most recently traveled to the People's Republic of China and to Moscow with President Nixon.

His second book, *A Very Personal Presidency: Lyndon B. Johnson in the White House* was published in July 1966.

Sidey is married to the former Anne Trowbridge of Columbia, Missouri, and they have three daughters and one son.